Praise for Energize Your Leadership

The power of storytelling comes alive in this collaborative book, *Energize Your Leadership*. These diverse leadership pros wisely decided to write a book that reached instead of preached. They dug deep into years of personal experiences to offer every leader and future leader the ONE thing they each need: A reflective way to stay energized. Without lecturing or proclaiming there is one best practice, they break through the apathy that all leaders can intermittently feel, with stories that inspire.

 - Kate Nasser, The People Skills Coach™

Energize Your Leadership is packed with insight and is one of the most exciting and innovative books on how to grow your personal leadership. A "must read" for any professional seeking proven techniques to achieve breakthroughs in their performance.

 - Steve Gutzler President, Leadership Quest

Energize Your Leadership is a truly inspirational, deeply compassionate, and perfectly practical book! Written by a group of experienced coaches and thought leaders, it teaches you how to lead with grounded authenticity and enlightened energy. It will inspire you to stand your ground, while respecting and serving others, to be creative and seek novel, practical solutions, and to use

your unique gifts and talents to overcome challenges and move forward with positive purpose. A Must Read!
  - Melanie Greenberg, PhD, Clinical Psychologist and Author

The lessons shared *Energize Your Leadership* not only inspire us to recognize our full potential, but it paves the way for us to become the kind of leader our employees need us to be. By sharing their own unique stories and experiences, the contributors to "Energize Your Leadership" help us understand how energizing ourselves, those around us, our workplaces, and our collective future can ensure we're able to bring out the best in those around us by bringing out the best of ourselves to our leadership role.
  - Tanveer Naseer, MSc.

Energize Your Leadership is more than a book, it is a 21st Century Credo for today's and tomorrow's leaders to lead and serve others, in an increasingly uncertain and ambiguous world. The diverse group of authors refreshingly open up their hearts and selflessly share personal stories, lessons learned and recommended actions which will greatly enhance one's leadership abilities. A must read for aspiring, new and experienced leaders seeking to, as we say in the U.S. Marine Corps, "fire-up" their leadership abilities.
  - Raphael Hernandez, Lieutenant Colonel, United States Marine Corps

Energize Your Leadership

Energize Your Leadership
Discover,
Ignite,
Break Through

Energized Leaders, LLC

Published by Energized Leaders, LLC

ISBN 978-1507894910

Printed in the United States of America

FIRST EDITION

Cover design by Derek Murphy

Dedication

For online collaborators who will take risks to help others succeed

Table of Contents

Foreword

Every great boss I've ever had understood the remarkable power of energy, in individuals and in teams. These great bosses not only understood that power, but they acted to create a work environment that encouraged positive energy in every interaction every day.

Energy is a vital quality - at work and outside of work - that is present when people are engaged, enthused, aligned, and valued.

The reality today, though, is that too few work environments generate positive energy, trust, and respect in daily interactions.

The research is sobering. A recent study by TinyHR [http://www.tinyhr.com/2014-employee-engagement-organizational-culture-report] found that 49% of employees are not satisfied with their direct supervisor. 66% of employees believe opportunities for professional growth are limited. Only 21% feel strongly valued at work (!).

It is likely that your experience matches the perceptions of these employees. Positive energy is not the norm in our lives, workplaces, or homes.

There is a better way - and this book provides actionable guidance to help your journey.

Chris Edmonds author of *The Culture Engine*

Introduction

Energize Your Leadership began as a collaboration among a group of leaders who met online with a dream to write a book about ways to ignite individual leadership. We came together around stories and experiences that had one theme in common: leaders were feeling sapped of energy. Somewhere along the way, these leaders had lost a sense of excitement—that feeling of being alive that powers everything you do. Some of us saw it in the workshops we were facilitating, others heard it from coaching clients; many of us noticed it in leadership at the organizations we worked at. No stranger to the phenomenon ourselves, we found that each of us had also experienced a moment or period of lack of excitement and energy. Wherever it was, we heard time and again how leaders were feeling overwhelmed, disengaged, and were searching for meaning. We saw that leadership was in need of a potent dose of energy.

Through online meet-ups, five content coaches created an outline for our vision of the book, while passionately discussing the most motivational ways to energize leaders. We began to notice a pattern: When a leader faced an energy crisis, it would oftentimes lead them to self-discovery and eventually to renewed accomplishment. From those conversations emerged a deeper understanding of the three steps leaders took to achieve growth and renewed energy: Discover, Ignite, Break Through. As the sections and chapters of the book came together, so did the friendships and personal stories for the coaches. We grew to understand what made each of us energized leaders and formed deep bonds to support our individual leadership journeys.

Eleven leadership experts from across the globe with diverse professional backgrounds and perspectives were then carefully selected based on their deep understanding of challenges leaders face. Each was asked to write a personal chapter telling the story of a struggle—as well as a powerful insight—that led them to energizing their leadership. The stories are all different, each revealing a moment of thought-provoking discovery. Each of the 16 stories herein highlights a different aspect of energized leadership. In collaborating with one another, all 16 authors developed extraordinary connections and friendships, creating a vibrant community of energized leadership.

The focus of the book is to understand how *energy* is a key driver for our individual leadership success. Since energy is the force that propels and moves things forward, when we become energized, we feel empowered to lead with passion and resilience. Our approach to exploring leadership is to journey from the *inside out*, so leaders first grasp who they are and what they stand for before connecting to and influencing others. It begins with an authentic look at oneself and moves outwards to touch the lives of those we encounter in our personal and professional worlds.

Energize Your Leadership is organized into four sections-—**Energize Yourself, Energize Others, Energize Your Workplace** and **Energize Your Future**. Each section speaks to an essential step in growing your leadership while revealing strategic ways to achieve individual breakthroughs. The four chapters in each section all follow the same three-part format:

- *The Story*
- *Lessons Learned*
- *Action Steps*

At the end of each chapter are specific action plans to put into place as well as questions to ask yourself to address the particular leadership theme. The book can be read sequentially or by choosing the topics that excite you first. Either way, the stories and lessons we learned will open your eyes to new leadership possibilities. We hope our book will help you to rekindle feeling alive again in your leadership with a strong sense of who you are and why you lead.

We invite you to explore with us how to *energize* your leadership—**Discover, Ignite, Break Through.**

The Content Coach Team

Chery Gegelman
Karin Hurt
Terri Klass
Alli Polin
LaRae Quy

Energize Your Leadership

Energize Yourself

Regardless of whichever philosophical or spiritual path you choose to follow, all of them have one factor in common – the root of all energy begins within, since the seed of all energy is found within ourselves. In this first part, we examine that seed by taking a look at four crucial energy centers found within ourselves and how best to tap them:

1. Values:

Values are the keys to our own motivations. They're what give us meaning, serving as our moral compass and emotional, ethical and social foundation. They dictate nearly all of our actions. Values have a kinetic energy that action carries to the outside.

2. Gifts:

We are aware of the gifts and capabilities we possess, but many times remain unaware of entire set of additional gifts we have. Discovering our hidden gifts not only helps complete us but also generates an innovative energy all its own.

3. Self-Questioning:

All true growth is done through trial and error and the resulting (or proceeding/preceding) self-questioning of one's own assumptions and notions. The energy of new discoveries and the overturning of previously-held frameworks is the key to personal progress.

4. Creativity:

Creativity is one of the strongest forces available to us and to truly exploit its highest potential, we need to give ourselves permission to unleash our creativity without boundaries to see what such energy is capable of producing.

1: Energize Your Values

"Whose life am I going to live?"

It's a question I would confront many times in my early career, beginning the moment I went off to college. In high school, I had taken those career aptitude tests that identified which jobs would be a good fit for someone with my personality and interests. My intuition told me they were spot on. Yet, instead of pursuing one of those career paths, I allowed my choices to be driven by the well-meaning, and seemingly wiser, voices of those around me. Intellectually, they made a lot more sense than what I intuitively felt would be a good fit for me.

I have no doubt that those well-meaning voices had my best interests at heart. I consider myself fortunate to have been surrounded by people who truly loved me, believed in me, and cared about my future. For a while, their guidance seemed to be working. My job was going very well. I had the time, energy and funds to enjoy doing things I loved to do. By all accounts I had a great life and a successful career.

Then one day a deceptively simple conversation jolted me awake. A friend at work shared over lunch that he was leaving the company to go to chiropractic school. Even though we were only in our twenties, it seemed like an incredibly gutsy move, one that required courage and insight.

When I asked him what drove his decision, he explained that he wanted his life to be "more than about crunching numbers and getting promotions." He genuinely wanted to help people lead healthier lives.

I didn't sleep much that night. Although I really enjoyed my job, his words somehow re-awakened my desire for my work and my life to have more meaning.

It became clear that at some point I had surrendered my quest for meaning, and had instead chosen to follow the path that had been laid out before me for as long as I could remember: go to school and get a good corporate job. "You can rise to the level I could never attain," my father had said, "because I did not get that degree." I was the first person in my family to graduate from college and with it came great hope and possibility for my entire family.

Over the next 10 years I explored many alternative careers, but I was continually frustrated that I still seemed unable to find the "right path." Did such a thing even exist? Perhaps I was expecting too much. I wasn't miserable or rudderless, and I didn't regret any of the choices I had made up until this point. It was just that something had been missing — the spark that made me want to seize the day, every day.

After years of searching for the "right" career path I had one of those aha moments: the meaning and satisfaction I was searching for had nothing to do with what I did for a living. I realized that the source of meaning and satisfaction came from the inside out, not the outside in. It wasn't a career I was seeking, but rather a compass to help me navigate. The thing I had been searching for was within my grasp the whole time — the compass was my values.

In that moment I had a clear choice: I could make my life one entirely of my own making or continue letting others drive my choices. I wanted my life to be my own, and I realized that the key was to get in touch with what really mattered to me. Fortunately, I had a strong personal code of ethics so my values at the level of my integrity were clear. Yet there was another set of values I needed to explore — the values that were the source of my motivations, behavior and satisfaction. It was in discovering these values that opened the door to understanding what gave me both meaning and satisfaction. The clearer I became about what these values were, the more energized I became about my future. I now had the tools to invent my life and career from this moment forward with confidence. I could find a way to make the difference I wanted to make in the world, and to live my whole life in a way that truly energized me.

LESSONS LEARNED

Only I can identify my values

Ultimately, this quest led me to realize that the real source of success and satisfaction comes down to one thing: living 100% true to your values in everything you do. This requires awareness, willingness and courage. Only you (not others) can identify and name your values. They must resonate on the deepest level of your being. When you do the work to distinguish your core values they will serve as a compass – an invaluable tool you can rely on to guide you in making decisions that bring you the most meaning, sense of purpose and satisfaction.

Distinguishing and learning to use your values as a compass can take time. Don't rush it or expect to create it overnight. This requires inquiry and self-discovery, after all. Take it day by day, and step by step. Over time I began to find that if I focused just on the step in front of me, trusting that the next step would reveal itself, I couldn't help but travel in the right direction. As long as I made my choices based on my values, I would be putting myself on that "right path" I had been seeking. Of course, I made mistakes and had setbacks along the way. That's all part of the process. Sometimes I got off track by unwittingly following the advice of others even though I knew better. Yet by being aware, I learned from my mistakes, corrected course, and got better at remembering to check in with my inner compass.

Being clear on what matters most energizes me

The ultimate litmus test for whether the choices I made were best serving me was the effect those choices had on my energy. When I was not experiencing being energized for a seemingly long stretch of time, my values became the compass for adjusting my course until that energy and enthusiasm for my work returned. In those times when I wanted to quit I looked to my core values to determine whether I simply needed to step up and charge through or whether it was time to correct course.

Once you can see clearly how values-driven decisions in your past led to an energized state, you have opened the door to exploring how you can leverage that awareness to consciously design your life to consistently experience being energized.

My values can optimize my contribution to my career and the world

The more I tuned in, I realized that my values drove my emotional responses to the world around me. I was able to design my career and my life to leverage the best of what I had to offer. This understanding has allowed me to choose how, where, and with whom I work and live in a way that has increased my sense of satisfaction in everything I do. Said another way, clarifying my values was the key to aligning who I am, what matters most to me, and the difference I want to make in the world.

It's important to remember that even when you live true to your values, you will experience challenges and obstacles. In fact, it can take great courage and fortitude to honor your values when the people around you, no matter how well-meaning, are pressing you to choose otherwise. Making choices based on your core values can give you the fortitude to work things through to get to the other side of whatever obstacles you face. That alone is a valuable form of energy that is essential to fueling your success and satisfaction in life and work.

Living true to your core values is not always the easy path, yet ultimately it is a path that allows you to create a life of meaning, satisfaction, purpose and abundant energy.

KEY QUESTIONS

- Which of your values are satisfied by your current job or career, and which are not?

- What could you do to satisfy a value that is not satisfied in your life?

- If you were to bring your whole self (with all your values) to work tomorrow, what might you do differently?

ACTION STEPS

Your core values are the elements in your life that you find most important, those that must be satisfied for you to feel that your life has meaning, that you're centered, and that you have energy and optimism. In determining your core values, it's helpful to look at your past decisions and experiences.

1. Take an inventory

Remember a work or life situation in which you experienced being energized by what you were doing. Write the story of what you were doing, why you were doing it, and what made it so energizing. Reflect on the story and identify the three values — those that are most important to you — that were satisfied through this experience. Repeat this exercise every day for the next seven days.

2. Enlist the help and perspective of others

Ask someone who believes in you and is supportive of your dreams to give feedback on your stories. Read them your stories and discuss together how your core values drove your choices, and the impact they had on your satisfaction and energy. Others may see things that you can't, and give you new insights. You can also ask someone who knew you as a child or young adult to tell you a story about when they witnessed you being the most joyful and energized.

3. Build your compass

You may notice in these exercises that certain values come up again and again. Pay special attention to these — they are your primary driving values, and figure most prominently on your values as a compass. They will give you the best guidance for making work and life decisions that give you meaning, purpose and a consistent sense of being energized.

By: Susan Mazza

www.RandomActsofLeadership.com

"The choice to live true to your values in everything you do is essential to energizing your leadership. #EnergizedLeaders"

2: Unwrap Your Gifts

In this age of strengths-finders and skills-focused thinking, leaders can spend an enormous amount of time focusing on what experience and skills they lack rather than taking stock of their existing knowledge and strengths. This can lead to seeing others as more skilled or talented than we are in our own areas of expertise. Sometimes we lack confidence in our abilities to tackle obstacles because we don't have a clear understanding of our own resources. That is exactly what happened to me when I was hired to present a series of training programs to a group of employees at a small manufacturing company.

The project consisted of designing and facilitating workshops on effective communication and team building. These are areas I have a great deal of experience with and love to present. The president of the organization was looking forward to offering her employees the workshop, and while she and I discussed the project, she said, "We have a great group of dedicated people, but English isn't the first language for many of them. In fact, there are often three different languages being spoken on the manufacturing floor at any given time."

My heart sank. I am not remotely fluent or even proficient in any other language except English. How was I going to be able to do anything with a group that couldn't understand me? What would such a communication program even look like if participants weren't able to follow my presentation? I didn't have the skills or knowledge to navigate such a diverse classroom.

As I tried to keep my rising panic at bay, I asked the president how she would like the workshops to be filled. She said, "Let's mix up all the managers and employees and all the backgrounds. If we run into language obstacles, we can have them translate for each other – they often do this on the floor so we can have them do it when they're with you."

Was this really going to happen? With shaky confidence, I set to work. I designed my programs with a focus on large, clear visuals and exaggerated fonts. I chose directions that were clear and exciting. I had my "plan" all ready and the day came for my first presentation.

I walked into the classroom, smiling and trembling. My first participants began to arrive, chatting in their different languages. I greeted everyone with enthusiasm and asked them to take a seat around a large oval conference table. They barely fit.

As I began my presentation (trying to remember to breathe), I noticed something quite amazing – the room was full of smiles and eagerness. The employees were thrilled to be there and be learning. Even when they didn't exactly understand the concepts, I was able to connect with their enthusiasm and help them build communication strategies. I used non-verbal forms such as visuals, charades, gestures – and they all not only understood, but reciprocated. Whenever there was confusion about a concept I offered or an idea or opinion a participant shared, someone always stepped in and translated as needed.

The change taking place in the room was just as powerful as the change taking place in me. A half-hour into the workshop I dumped my "plan" and decided to just have fun, and facilitate the workshop in a way that felt organic. When it came time to create a Coat of Arms for the company, many of the groups drew pictures of a family working together. That's how they saw themselves in their work worlds – an interconnected team of employees working in a nurturing and respectful environment. The energy in the room was palpable – we were all invigorated by the collaboration and learning. Bringing my strength of facilitation to the fore had enabled this group to forge new connections and better communication. Collectively, we were a hive of creative activity and innovation.

I had made assumptions about my skills and capabilities as well as my limitations but on this day, I was put in a situation where my supposed skills were of limited use. This gave me the unexpected opportunity to use alternative methods and techniques – ones that I might not have otherwise chosen. And that is when I discovered that my skills in facilitation, communications, and connecting with people and hearing their concerns and ideas was my gift because I had so many more ways of accomplishing this than I had previously thought. This discovery made all the difference in how I saw myself and how I related to others. It empowered me to be the best trainer I could be – one whose effectiveness wasn't dependent on the specific design of a workshop or the backgrounds of the workshop's participants. To this day, if ever I feel vulnerable in a presentation, I tap into the energy that's always available to me when I remember to just allow my gifts to shine.

How many leaders and others rely on a fixed set of strengths and never venture outside of their safety zones to discover new ones? If it were not for the fact that I put myself in an uncomfortable position where I apparently lacked the resources I so heavily relied on, I might have never discovered these newfound skills.

LESSONS LEARNED

We all experience unexpected and imperfect conditions in our leadership journeys. Whether we are dealing with a work force with communication barriers, a challenging project or a slowdown in our consulting practices, we need to ask ourselves how we can use our talents and gifts to enable a positive outcome. Understanding what strengths and knowledge each of us brings to our work and careers can revitalize us and propel us forward.

Our gifts are the strengths that come naturally

When I thought about how to best overcome my anxiety about not understanding the participants and them not understanding me, I played to my natural style. I called upon my innate trait of being approachable and nurturing. Although I've been a corporate trainer for many years, I didn't always recognize these gifts. I'd known I could design effective training programs, but that didn't always excite me. This experience allowed me to dig deep and recognize that my natural ability to be genuine and challenge trainees in a meaningful way was an "ace" in my toolbox.

Thinking about how best to engage the participants automatically triggered my ability to connect with them. And my natural curiosity about people and their challenges further facilitated that connection. The particulars of the program structure became less critical, and instead I focused on empowering others to be their best by finding their unique talents. This made me feel more alive, energized the presentation, and inspired the workshop participants, bringing them to new levels of learning and collaboration.

Our toolkit of gifts and resources can make a difference

Each of us possesses a set of strengths and experiences that can be used as tools to make the greatest impact. For example, my gift for connecting with and empowering trainees made all the difference in facilitating a successful workshop.

I needed to believe in my facilitation skills and abilities to engage people to effect change. I *did* have the tools I needed to effectively work with this population. It was simply a matter of recognizing and trusting them, and using them wisely. When we start discovering our overlooked gifts, we see that we have an entire toolbox at our disposal. Sometimes, you'll even find that tools can come from others. In my case, the president of the company gave guidance that proved immeasurably helpful – that diverse languages wouldn't impact the success of my training.

Focus on strengths instead of blind spots

We react too quickly to saying what we don't know how to do as opposed to identifying what we excel at and how those strengths can lead us to change and growth. To be successful with these workshops, I needed to focus on what I excelled at, not all the skills I thought I was lacking. I needed to worry less about the design of the program and more about what how I could create a dynamic community within the conference room. When we recognize but don't dwell on our blind spots, we are more able to embrace who we are. This allows us to "play up" our gifts for the greatest impact.

Maybe you head up a small firm or you're a team member in a large company, or maybe you're a solo entrepreneur. Wherever you lead from, you can energize your leadership if you are willing to discover and share your unique capabilities, knowledge and gifts.

KEY QUESTIONS

- What talents and strengths do you bring to your professional and personal worlds?

- What might people say are your strengths or natural gifts?

- How can you put your gifts and strengths into play?

ACTION STEPS

Beginning today, stop focusing on what skills you think you need to acquire and instead direct your exploration towards what you do really well. We become energized when we realize how much talent, experience and strength we bring to our lives and careers.

1. Discover your successes

Look back on the past few months and reflect on what activities or responsibilities brought you the most success and made you feel good about leading. Even if you are not a manager or have any particular title, you are influencing and impacting those around you.

The idea is not to label yourself but rather think of those activities that energize you and that others appreciate you doing. Those skills, knowledge or expertise tend to be our natural strengths and gifts.

2. Identify your gifts

Looking at these successes, create a list of five gifts that stand out for you. These tend to be the various traits that, when employed, lead to successes. For example, some of us are analytical and enjoy working with data to solve problems. Others are creative and feel happiest when they're able to innovate and apply outside-the-box thinking. Still others are great listeners and can synthesize auditory information and make sense of it for a collaborative effort.

3. Ask for input

We call them blind spots for a reason. When trying to determine your own gifts that you might not recognize, it can be helpful to enlist the help of others for their perspective. Meet with colleagues, bosses, friends or collaborators to discuss your strengths. When you hear what other people say about your abilities, make sure to honor the words and receive the feedback openly. Finally, choose two or three gifts that you can start sharing right away.

By: Terri Klass

www.terriklassconsulting.com

"When we play to our gifts, we feel more alive in our leadership. #EnergizedLeaders"

3: Question Yourself

Some people say that the two greatest days of your life are the day you were born and the day you discovered why. You wouldn't be reading this if you hadn't achieved that first day, but the second one – well, that's one that often eludes us. So much has been written and spoken about the *why* that drives us. The big *why* fuels the mental, emotional, physical and even spiritual horsepower that drives what we've done and what we strive to do. It underlies our purpose, passion and things we resonate with and embrace. But it goes deeper than that: Many times we embark on finding our why only after we've lost the energy it once provided us.

I had been working for a successful and well known civil contractor for about eleven years. I had moved up in the company fairly rapidly and was enjoying what I had been doing as well as the people I had been doing it with. Much of my time had been spent on jobsites and I remember feeling much gratitude and fulfillment for being recognized as someone who had led their team to completing their part of the project on time and within budget. I had thought I had found my dream job – everything seemed to be going so well.

In the spring of 2009, I learned that the man that I had worked for over the last eleven years had been diagnosed with an untreatable form of cancer. Four months later, he was gone and I found myself working for six bosses instead of one.

During the transitional period following the passing of my boss, my job description changed significantly. My duties in the field, working with "my guys," had all but been eliminated, and my new role had me pretty much relegated to my four-wheel, ergonomically correct, office cruiser (i.e. – my office chair).

For ten or twelve hours a day, I was thinking about the way things had been and wondering why I felt so lost, so out of energy. Somewhere along the way, I had lost that spark – the spark that had inspired me to get it done, no matter what it took. Somehow my work life had turned into one of dreading deadlines and wondering how long I could sustain myself under these conditions.

It hadn't always been like this.

Throughout my career, I had enjoyed and embraced various leadership roles but none of them were by design. I never had any special training and truthfully had read very little about the topic of leadership – I simply found fulfillment in adding value to others. My happiest and most energized times at work were when I was helping others to succeed, encouraging them when they needed it, and creating opportunities for them to better themselves. Leadership had come so naturally to me, that I didn't question it.

The majority of my professional life had been spent outside of the walls of what most consider the "office." I had become a product of my environment and when the environment changed I was unable to change with it. Normal wasn't normal anymore and as hard as I wanted to figure it out and feel the joy I had once experienced, I just could not find that sweet spot.

I still had a great salary, benefits and perks. The problem was that none of those things had been filling my bucket. Even worse, I did not even know where my buckets were.

Now you might think that I had realized what was going on this entire time, but I didn't. I didn't get it. I had still been getting things done. I was still successful in achieving my work goals. But something was not right and I knew I needed to figure out what had changed. My lack of awareness, compounded by the fact that I had become disconnected from who I was, left me believing that the only option I had was to find a completely new environment.

Choosing to leave the only thing I knew for the previous thirty years was the decision I made and it took two grueling years to come out on the other side. I was lucky. I found my "next" and recognize that even though I am doing something completely different now, it didn't have to be that way. Although I don't have regrets, I know that if I'd been connected to my why, if I'd started questioning earlier, I may not have had to undergo such a grueling transition.

Questioning yourself is not an easy task and it's one we all would rather avoid because routine and all that is familiar is comforting – even if superficially. It's not that we are not aware that there can be better out there, it's our fear of stepping outside what is familiar. It takes a lot of energy to question, but it also releases a lot of energy in a positive sense when you take the steps that come with questioning.

LESSONS LEARNED

Focus on who you are, not what you do

In hindsight, my journey could have gone much differently. I realize now that it was because I found my identity in what I did, rather than in who I was. When what I did changed, my identity was lost and I struggled to find the energy I once had. As leaders, we have to make sacrifices. We put others first and find success in the success of those we lead. I had become a leader with no followers and totally missed it when it happened. The "why" that once fueled me had been lost and I was literally running on empty. I had become consumed by tasks and projects; that I'd disconnected from who I was.

Don't forget to take care of yourself

After working with other leaders over the last three years, I've noticed an all-too familiar pattern. Leaders, by nature, have a tendency to disengage from their tribe when they become too busy taking care of everyone else to take care of themselves. Our "why" as a leader becomes lost when we start focusing solely on the why that drives others. I believe the breakdown or disengagement comes from losing focus on the real purpose of leadership. When the why that provides you energy is compromised, your ability to lead is also compromised. Leaders who remember to take care of themselves have teams that are empowered, energized and focused on impactful work.

Empowering others energizes you

I look back on what went right during my tenure in the world of construction and can now say that what filled me up was setting others up for success. I didn't realize it at the time, but in doing so I was creating not followers, but leaders, and their success was my success.

If you want to be a great leader, you need to provide your people with opportunities and tools, but they need to execute the plan to achieve them. I had lost my group of people to lead and because of my own blindness, missed out on an entirely different group of people that could have benefitted from my leadership skills. But rather than see the opportunity, I chose to start solving others' problems. Rather than empowering, I was enabling and because of that, my road to burnout began.

We can motivate and inspire, but at the end of the day, it is up to the individual to perform. The minute we choose to become personally responsible for someone's success, we take on the burden of their performance. Set them up for success and they are much more likely to succeed; and like I have suggested, you will feel the success in what they accomplish. Identifying and focusing on a collective why is how you get energized as a leader.

You will also build on the relationships you have. Part of your purpose as a leader should be to create a culture in which your team is working within their WHY. Give them ownership in what they are working on and allow them to be part of the process. Not only will this empower them, but it will increase their desire to be an active participant in problem solving and reduce yours. If there is one thing I am sure of when it comes to the purpose of a leader, it's that you are only going to find it by discovering the why that energizes your people and the organization. Organizations need to focus on a collective why in order to maintain clarity and focus on the most important goals.

KEY QUESTIONS

- What would it take to increase your level of awareness?

- What intention have you set to create a change?

- Who could you ask to hold you accountable in achieving your goals?

ACTION STEPS

1. **Ask powerful questions**

In the most basic of terms, you don't know what you don't know. And until you know what that is, you will be unable to make any changes that will benefit you or your team. Start to ask yourself, and your team, powerful questions. All your discussions should revolve around asking questions. This is where change comes from. I love the quote, "if you keep doing what you've been doing, you'll keep getting what you've been getting." Does this resonate?

2. Create a change

Don't accept the way things are as being okay just because they have always been that way. Ask, "How can we make ourselves better?" or "How can we do what we do better?" and guide your team in finding the solution.

3. Be accountable

It's pretty simple: if you could have done it yourself, you would have already done it. Share your goals with someone and have them hold you accountable to achieving them. Take it a step further and set up an accountability program for your people.

By: Barry Smith

www.buildingwhatmatters.com

"A strong enough WHY will always reveal the HOW" *#EnergizedLeaders*

4: Unleash Your Creativity

Something almost divine attracted me to an event a few years ago: a local artist was giving a talk on the tremendous success he enjoyed after taking creative action on a serendipitous idea. The timing couldn't have been better. I had been stuck in a rut and was in need of something to re-energize me and put me back on track. Creative inspiration might be just the thing. I signed up immediately.

On the day of the talk, I'd come down with a nasty head cold and the thought of curling up in bed under the covers sounded far more appealing than trudging outside to then sit in a room full of people for a presentation. But I felt obliged to show up for at least part of the event, so I bundled up and made my way to the venue.

Despite the miserable cold, I was glad I'd come out. The artist's presentation was fantastic—visually engaging and packed with incredible insights. I filled my Moleskin pages as quickly as I could, trying to keep up with my ideas and inspirations.

Until . . . about 30 minutes into the session, when the artist wrapped up his formal presentation and told us that the rest of the evening would be devoted to a hands-on exercise. Huge sigh. I was ill: the last thing I wanted to do was think, work or interact with other humans.

Convinced I'd received all the insight I was going to get, I decided it was the perfect time to slip out unnoticed. Besides, who would mind if the sneezing nose-blower left?

Unfortunately, I took too long weighing my options and was now was stuck as our leader explained the assignment instructions. Our first task was to collect a bunch of trash items from a rather large pile mounded on top of an oak table. We were instructed to pick a shape, a simple shape—like a circle or square. I chose a triangle. Using only the trash from the table, we had an hour to craft *at least* 45 images of our shape.

And before I knew it, we were off.

I timed it—I needed to create a new shape every 90 seconds or so. *Phew, that's fast!* To make matters worse, my first two triangles took almost ten minutes! I realized I needed to speed things up. Pretty soon, I couldn't tell if the sweat on my forehead was from the cold or the pace, but I was definitely in a groove. After completing a few more, an interesting transition took place: I started to focus less on the quality of my creations and more on how quickly I could produce them. I grabbed whatever material was in front of me and fashioned a new design as quickly as I could, in a seemingly unconscious manner, and then proceeded onto the next. I became a speed demon!

I opened my mind, relaxed my inner judge, and before I knew it, the hour was up and I had filled the wall with 52 triangles! I took a step back (and a deep breath) and proudly looked at my accomplishment. While there were many clunkers among the 52, there were some really interesting creations that even received recognition from my classmates. My feeling of dread suddenly transformed into pride!

Looking at that wall, letting my eyes move slowly over those triangles (and all the other shapes), I realized some things. Most importantly, changing one's perspective is crucial for unleashing creativity.

Being a creature of habit not only affects us cognitively, but behaviorally. Think about how often we get stuck in the same old routines: taking the same driving route to work, getting the same cup of coffee from the same Starbucks at the same time, and spending our day in the same conference room or behind our desk. Sameness is no friend of creativity; sameness only safeguards the status quo.

Our desks, in fact, might be the worst place to try to find inspiration. To unleash our creativity, we must take responsibility to create the time to experience life outside the office. This doesn't necessarily mean hopping on a plane, it just means we should get away from the computer and do things that are thought-provoking and that stimulate curiosity.

Getting out of our comfort zone and changing perspective will do wonders for allowing more creative stimuli to inspire the imagination. Ask a colleague to join you at a museum and explore all the exhibits together. Go check out a building known for its innovative architecture, or go visit a start-up retail business and ask the owner about her vision and how it came to fruition. Put yourself in new, interesting and creative places and really absorb all there is to see, feel and hear.

The most important aspect of these expeditionary trips is to link our observations back to business. Ask deep questions that invite curiosity. Why are they doing this? How did they do it? What's the implication for *our* business? How can we apply this insight? When we ask these questions, we're essentially challenging the brain to make connections and create context; many times this is all that's needed to invite new ideas.

We're all creative beings. Our brains are hard-wired to perform in this magical capacity. The wonderful thing about creativity is that it is regenerative and infinitely abundant. So, even if you haven't engaged creatively in some time, don't worry! You haven't lost your ability by any means. Shut off the mental chatter and inner judge, and allow your five senses to receive the inspiration that surrounds you all day, every day. Creativity has an extraordinary ability to magically reappear—you just need to create a space for it and be willing to follow.

And remember: there's no such thing as "feeling ready." Painter Chuck Close once said, "Inspiration is for amateurs—the rest of us just show up and get to work." Relying on perfect conditions as a precursor to begin work will only result in procrastination. There's no better time like the present to start something new. Sure, it may feel like a struggle to get going, but once pen is put to paper, the mind will break free from its lethargy and will flourish with creative ideas. And when you unleash creativity, you unleash energy.

LESSONS LEARNED

Creativity can be fickle. Sometimes it's just there, other times it needs to be coaxed into the light. The latter was certainly the case for me when I began the triangle exercise. By the end of the experience, I had a heck of a lot more than just 52 pictures of triangles; I learned some vital lessons about creativity:

Let go of precision and perfection

I've come to realize that I often wait for ideal conditions because I've set too high a bar for quality. This traps me into thinking that ideas must be brilliant before I can act on them. It doesn't take long before my ego dismisses my creative notions as folly, or tries to convince me that someone else already did something similar—only better. Nothing kills creativity faster than ridicule from our inner judge. I've learned that I must let go of the need to judge my ideas so harshly. Now I focus on output; get all the ideas out of my head and onto paper so that they can be shared with others. It's the sharing that's so critically important and where the true magic of precision and perfection takes place.

The best ideas are rarely the first ones

After completing the exercise, the artist asked us a critical question: "At what point did you create your best image?" We all realized our best images came deep into the exercise, after our creative mind was unfettered. In business we're all constrained by time and too often, just for expediency's sake, accept the first idea that comes along. Imagine what could be achieved if our teams had adequate time to really explore and experiment. Why not give them a chance to discover that their 18th idea is a home run!

Be wary of habits and faulty assumptions

We all have a perspective of how the world operates, a set of assumptions that influence our behavior and decision-making. The challenge is that these assumptions become so ingrained that they form mental blinders, which prevent us from accurately appraising the value or utility of something novel. When unique ideas cannot be clearly processed, we're inclined to dismiss them. When I thought, "What possible value can I gain from making triangles out of trash?" I was rejecting the concept because I had no prior experience that suggested it would be productive. That's the key lesson: don't let your assumptions trick you into thinking there's nothing to gain from experiencing something new. A truly novel idea won't seem familiar or safe. As author John Hunt reminds us, "The gap between what you already know and what you're exploring is often when the best ideas pop up."

KEY QUESTIONS

- How does your inner-judge impact your decision-making when it comes to evaluating new ideas?

- How can your leadership provide others the time and space for creative thinking?

- What local attractions can you take your team to that will inspire and invite curiosity?

ACTION STEPS

Expressing creativity is a choice. You don't need permission to think creatively or try new things. And you certainly shouldn't sit and wait until someone asks us to be creative. Make a commitment to invite creativity into your daily routine.

1. **Do the work (and drop the judgment!)**

Don't wait until you feel ready or inspired to be creative. There's no "right time" for creativity. Set aside the time to contemplate, then roll up your sleeves and take action. When you let go of perfection, precision and the inner judge, you'll see a surge in creative output.

2.   Search beyond the first good idea

There's a difference between the first good acceptable solution and a truly great, disruptive idea. The former is usually easy to discover, the latter almost always takes more time and exploration. Give yourself the time and space to go for the latter.

3.   Change your perspective and get inspired

Schedule regular time to get out of the office and stimulate your imagination. Remember, our desks are the worst place to get inspired. Go, wander, visit and contemplate. Ask thought-provoking questions: don't just observe, ask questions that invite curiosity and force the brain to make new connections.

By: Tony Vengrove

www.milesfinchinnovation.com

"Sameness is no friend of creativity; sameness only safeguards the status quo.
#EnergizedLeaders"

Energize Others

Energizing others begins with the self. When you deeply know your values and gifts, the next step is bringing that true self outward – with authenticity and honesty. A foundation of authenticity brings life, vigor and genuine connection to personal and professional relationships. From there, you can meet the needs of others and motivate them to be active participants in the co-creative process. In this section, we look at four practices key to people-energizing:

1.   True to Oneself:

Authenticity is key to connecting with and energizing others, but it can only come about if one is authentic with oneself. If a leader is not honest with him or herself, any attempt at authenticity with others is doomed.

2. Being Seen for What (and Who) You Are:

Energy comes from a source and it is essential that leaders project themselves in such a way that is both honest and authentic. When a leader is authentic and shows up as their true self, their employees will be compelled and energized to do likewise.

3. Deal with Problem People:

Nothing disrupts the flow of energy in the workplace quite like problem people, but there are ways in which a leader can harness the negative energy that problem people generate and transform it into a positive force.

4. Serve to Lead. Lead to Serve:

Leadership is energized as much by giving of yourself as by receiving from others. When leadership begins with service and is built on trust it energizes both the leader and the follower.

5: Being Authentic to Others (and Yourself)

I had just been promoted to my first big leadership position in Human Resources, concurrent with a significant merger with a major Fortune 500 company. All the "important" players were new: I had a new boss, a new team and new senior leaders to impress. And because life is messy sometimes, I also was going through a divorce and trying to pick up the pieces in a new life, while getting settled in a new home . . . as a single mom. The job required substantial travel to Manhattan – and I lived in Baltimore.

One of the first tasks in my new role was to build a Diversity strategy. We gathered a diversity council representing each business unit to collaborate on the strategy and plans. The work we were doing was vital. I was convinced I was nailing my new role. Until . . .

"You're a fraud!"

One of the council members had burst into my office, pointed her finger at me and yelled her accusation. I was stunned. I couldn't imagine what she was talking about. Her words really stung too, given that she was a trusted teammate. She motioned towards my desk, "I came by your office yesterday when you weren't here and saw the pictures on your desk. They are all of you and your son—no Dad. You lead all these meetings on making it easier for single moms and NOT ONE TIME do you mention that you are one. What else aren't you sharing?"

She got me. But I had an explanation—a justified spin!—but as hard as I tried to get the words out, there was no legitimate way to explain.

The truth is, I had been very deliberate about keeping my messy life circumstance hidden. Even my new boss did not know what I was going through. I had heard enough discussion about single moms needing "extra care and support" to reduce absenteeism and remain productive. I thought, ***I'm*** *not like that. I'm a* ***different*** *kind of single mom.* I'm an Executive, with a capital "E."

I'd been in enough closed-door discussions to know that although such circumstances shouldn't matter, they can easily lead to subtle biases that make someone else a "better fit." I was certain that if my secret came out, the decision makers would question my ability to travel. Not to mention doubting the credibility of a HR leader who couldn't even keep her marriage together.

Suddenly I realized how absurd this all sounded, even to myself.

I began checking around with some other folks on the council. One gay man said, "Karin, you work so hard to get to know us as people and we love that. We all trusted you with some pretty big stuff. But, we're starting to wonder about you. You know all about us, but we know nothing about you. We're not sure we can trust you."

With his words, I felt a pang of shame. Not because of who I was, but because I had hidden it. I had achieved a position, but had lost the trust of my followers. I had been given a beautiful opportunity to use my life as an example of what a single mom could achieve; to face subtle discrimination head-on and be the voice of those who did not yet have a seat at the table.

Instead, I checked true courage at the door, put up the walls and protected myself . . . all the while creating a diversity strategy that I convinced myself (and others) was game-changing.

I had the title, but was not a leader in action. My inability to be authentic with myself and with others led to a breakdown in communications and trust and being labeled (unfortunately yet correctly) as a fraud. Seeing this clearly inspired me to change the way I showed up as a leader, forever.

Being authentic doesn't mean that you have to follow a prescribed set of rules of behavior, but it does mean you have to be open and communicative about who you are as a person and your actions as a leader. Being authentic about shortcomings or limitations is not, as many would believe, something that kills your influence or leadership. If anything, sharing that information with others (as well as your own discomforts with yourself) can actually help your leadership efforts.

Turns out inauthenticity saps energy, resources and morale. In short, inauthenticity is expensive

– for the organization, for efficiency, for your energy. It encourages game-playing,... I found out, after "coming out," that my life, leadership style, and relationships changed, and I was energized.

Leaders should promote and demonstrate authenticity and reciprocal authenticity as necessary for all relationships. Authenticity is what builds trust and ultimately proves to be the currency of engagement for all leaders, but this authenticity to others also requires an authenticity with oneself.

The challenge we face as leaders is to adopt vulnerability as a permanent component of leadership. In the decade and a half after that pivotal moment, I've had many successes and blessings, both personally and professionally. I've also had some setbacks, of course. I don't have this thing totally handled. But that's just the territory of leadership: showing up as your authentic self, and doing the best you can.

LESSONS LEARNED

Relationships require reciprocal disclosure

Building connected and committed relationships requires a two-way exchange of real. It's not enough to just get to know your people. They yearn to know more about you as well. They want to know they are following a human being who understands that life is messy and that work isn't always easy. The more they get you, the more they will let you see them.

And remember – BS is obvious. No matter how fancy the spin, people can spot inauthenticity in a flash. Sure they may play along, particularly if you're the boss, but if you're holding back, they can tell. This can create an atmosphere of "us versus them," and encourage needless gossip or talking behind backs.

Inauthenticity is expensive

Inauthenticity also drains energy and has huge costs on immediate results, lasting impact, health and families. Trying to lead like someone else, or spin the truth, will wear you down and make you cranky. When you spend time working to show up differently that who you are, to win the game and keep up a facade, you waste precious energy that could be invested in creating breakthrough vision, developing people and working on the work.

Game playing is contagious

Teams sense you're playing games, they'll spend time working to figure out the rules rather than working on the work. In fact, they'll be taking notes to learn to play the game too.

All that contagious facade building pulls hearts and minds from the important mission at hand. If they sense it's better to show up looking "perfect" than authentic, they'll follow that lead.

The more ambitious folks on your team are also watching how you handle all the pressure of your position. Do you stay true to your core values, or are you being groomed to be someone else?

Authenticity is tricky because we're in a constant state of discovery of who we are and how we relate to the world. The most energized leaders I know invest deeply in this process.

KEY QUESTIONS

- When do you feel most authentic in your leadership?

- What one or two behaviors could you change to show up more real for you? For your team? For your boss?

- How do you encourage and reward authentic

ACTION STEPS

1. Know yourself

Be constantly curious about your leadership and the impact you are making, both good and bad. Have a good understanding of your own strengths and weaknesses. Don't pretend to be someone you are not. Admit your weaknesses and how you are working to improve on them. Seek out feedback and act on it. Surround yourself with people who will tell you the truth.

Only when you know yourself, can you *be* yourself. Be true to your leadership values and style. Avoid emulating someone else's style to fit a certain mold. Strive for integration and consistency of who you are across various contexts (e.g., work, home, church). Conduct a regular "authenticity audit" Notice the times where you feel energized and excited to be whom you truly are. Also notice when you feel like you're playing a part or wearing a mask. If it helps, keep a list. No one feels at the top of their game all the time, but it's important to notice your energy patterns. What situations bring out the best and most authentic parts of you? Which don't?

2. Say what's true

Be trustworthy and honest. Do what you say. Don't withhold information. Be willing to have the tough conversations. This doesn't mean blurting out every thought or being insensitive to others. After all, your truth is a truth, but not necessarily the only truth. Say what you mean with great care and an authentic desire to improve the scene and to support the people in it.

3. Commit to something bigger than yourself

Be committed to the mission at a deep level. If your heart's not in it, consider your motives. Doing what's right trumps any personal agenda. Nothing zaps authenticity faster than a leader who feels trapped in a role they no longer believe in. The best energy comes from deep intrinsic motivation to the work at hand.

Be genuinely interested in other people as humans, not just for what they can do to make your life easier. Make extra effort to connect at a deeper level up, down and sideways. This will feel scary. Do it anyway. Your team wants to know who you are, and most importantly they want to be truly seen for who they are. And yes, deep down, so does your boss, your suppliers, and your peers. Invest deeply in a lot of listening and a bit of disclosure. Talk about more than just the work. It works.

By: Karin Hurt

www.letsgrowleaders.com

"There is no greater gift you can give your team than leading from who you truly are, toward head-turning results. #EnergizedLeaders"

6: Be Seen for Who You Are

Many of us make necessary – or what we deem necessary – sacrifices to climb the corporate ladder and be seen as capable, intelligent, leaders. Often, this means playing it safe by suppressing parts of ourselves that make us special or unique, but may not be right for the workplace. For me, this began with clothing.

When I first started as a young female executive working for a Big Six consulting firm, there were strict do's and don'ts for our appearance and behavior:

- Do wear a suit with a matching jacket.

- Do not wear a pantsuit if you're a woman.

- Do go out to lunch.

- Do not go to a fast food restaurant.

The message here was explicit: you are a professional and professionals don't dress shabby and they don't frequent lower-end restaurants.

I quickly went from looking like a college student with long flowing hair, to a corporate professional, thanks to a small investment in the right wardrobe and a conservative haircut. I looked dramatically different on the outside, but was still me on the inside.

I was happy and successful as a management consultant on the rise. I enjoyed the added bonus of a reasonable commute . . . until the first winter, when severe ice storms hit and sidewalks became a hazard.

That's when I slipped on the ice and broke my wrist. One misstep, and everything changed.

Oddly (and incredibly telling), my biggest concern wasn't my injury, but was the fact that I couldn't fit my work blazer over my cast. I was afraid of what the leaders would think, but I had no other choice: I had to wear a sweater.

At first, I chose my most conservative sweaters, but as the days passed, I reached for ones that were a little more "me." I realized I could show a bit more of my true personality through my attire as long as the cast remained on my arm. I was afraid someone would say something, but no one did. That small choice of wearing some of my favorite sweaters led to my next small choice: wearing more earrings.

I had my ears pierced many times over the years, but always wore a single pair of small, appropriate studs to work. One day, I started wearing some extra hoops and wondered if anyone would notice or care. Almost immediately, a partner commented on my new look with disapproval, but did not request that I remove them. So I didn't.

These small actions actually helped me to show up in a different way. Not only was I working hard, but was also bringing more of myself to the job. I suddenly had more ease, energy and commitment to the work knowing I could be me – inside and out – *and* a management consultant. One did not have to preclude the other.

My heart felt full and life was good. But soon I hit a professional crossroads, and realized I wanted to take the next step to Vice President – a senior leader not only in tenure, but also in title.

I know we are not defined by our titles, but it still felt like hard-earned recognition of my knowledge, skills and abilities. I also knew that I had to play the corporate game to make the climb of a rising executive, so I returned to the suits and removed the extra earrings for good. It worked, and I made VP.

But attaining that coveted title was problematic because not being true to myself now extended to more than just clothing. I had two children and a husband, and yet the year I was promoted to VP I was away from home for my son's birthday, my birthday and my wedding anniversary.

My leadership team was on a tight deadline to deliver big results. Initially, I did what every leader is tempted to do: turn up the speed on the treadmill. There was no way I was going to jump off. I spent more time on airplanes, got savvy with analytics, and constantly checked in with my teams. I was juggling many (too many) balls between work and home, but I was not going to let anyone see me drop one.

And then, one night before a big meeting, I was going through some last minute preparations with my boss, when my phone rang and I took the call that jolted me awake.

My young daughter was on the other end, and she wanted me to come home for dinner and to tuck her into bed. It was a simple request; but I could not remember the last time I tucked her in on a week-night. I explained that even if I left for the airport right away, I could never make it home in time. Despite steeling myself against the disappointment, each of her sobs broke my heart a little more. I was not only letting her down, I was letting myself down.

Clearly, if I wanted to not only fix what had gone wrong, but also make things right going forward, I needed to change. I needed the courage to vulnerably show up as *all* of me, and not just the superstar VP who could do it all.

I was both a VP, *and* a mother and wife. The way I was living and working left me with little energy for anyone—my team, my husband, my children—but also not insignificantly: myself. I knew I had to break the frame I had so skillfully built not only to reconnect with my energy and heart, but also to shed the corporate mask that was my constant companion.

LESSONS LEARNED

There is an undeniable energy that comes from knowing and accepting yourself. You move from slogging through the muck of life to accepting that fear and possibility, hope and pain, doubt and preparation can all co-exist. Messy becomes OK because it's human.

Perfection and control are illusions that no one can live up to, and they certainly don't allow us to breathe deeply – or move freely – while under their weight. Honoring my commitment to change meant vulnerably casting off my armor to break through to my heart. You too can boldly and bravely be seen for who you are when you stop compartmentalizing your life and leadership.

Let people in

Much like my broken arm, my daughter's phone call was the impetus for new choices. To change, I needed to admit that I was falling short. That was incredibly hard, but also a turning point. I asked my husband for his support and talked to my friends who had been in similar circumstances: successful yet lost. I also exposed my truth when I talked to my boss about what would re-energize my leadership and ultimately benefit the team most. The more I admitted I was struggling, the stronger and more energized I became. Every time I spoke the truth it gave me permission to do it again and again, instead of hiding in fear that someone would notice I wasn't perfect.

What I saw over and over was that vulnerability paves the way for authentic connection instead of practiced perfection.

Energize through relationships

I'm a coach, people developer and relationship-focused leader, not a down-in-the-details process expert or spreadsheet guru. Spreadsheets zapped my energy, but having honest and vulnerable conversations where I didn't have all of the answers wasn't scary, it was energizing. Our program was struggling and we needed to talk about it, not ignore it. I kept my door open to discuss the hard truths, fears and challenges with the front line team, not only in closed door senior meetings.

I met my team members on a human-to-human level. No titles, no pretension, I laid it on the line with my team leads for our shared success and my sanity. They kept looking to me for answers and approval because my box was higher than theirs on the org chart. I honestly didn't want to be the authority on their job, I trusted them and needed them to step forward as the experts. I told them sincerely, "I need you. You are the leader." In that moment, all of our energy skyrocketed as I refused to do their job for them or without them.

Do not roll over in defeat

Contorting myself to fit the mold in a culture that didn't fit my leadership had taken a toll on my heart, happiness and health. I am a fighter and initially I thought defeat was not turning around our division fast enough. I now see that defeat was letting go of who I am in exchange for a seat at a table. The phone call from my daughter was a wakeup call to re-ignite, re-invent and re-engage in my whole life. My energy soared as I chose to fully be me for the first time in a very long time.

Being seen for who you are requires that you know who you are. I am an earring-wearing, sweater-loving coach, mother, wife, sister, friend, leader, innovator, change agent and possibilities junkie. It's easy to get lost in the climb, but only you can choose to be committed enough, brave enough and vulnerable enough to be you.

KEY QUESTIONS

- When was the last time you showed the real you at work?

- What scares you the most about letting down your guard?

- How would allowing others to see you for who you are energize your leadership?

ACTION STEPS

1.   Choose to be you and a success

It doesn't have to be an either-or choice. Small acts that enable you to break the frame of "leaders act like this, not that" will give you the energy to show up more fully.

Make time to brainstorm alone or with a partner for five minutes on ways that you can step out more boldly, authentically and vulnerably to break the frame today. Look at your list and pick the one thing that you will commit to actually doing.

2. Make vulnerable and courageous choices

It takes brave and intentional choices that are aligned with your core self to be seen for who you are – and not only your title. Starting today, make a choice every day (it can be tiny or massive) that aligns with who you really are. Be sure to notice what you're gaining (and what you're afraid of losing) by making those choices. Exercise your vulnerability muscle further by letting someone in on your greatest challenges.

3. Live your truth

When you always keep your fears, hopes, dreams and failings private, you're in essence hiding behind a wall of perfection that's impossible to maintain and sets a false bar for others in their own life and leadership. Reflect on some of the choices you've made from step #2 above – what are you saying YES to, and what are you saying NO to by letting others see you for who you are?

By: Alli Polin

www.breaktheframe.com

"Forget showing the world you're perfect. Show people that you're human. #EnergizedLeaders"

7: Speaking Up Around Problem People

Greg was angry when he came back into the office, and all 6'5" and 300 lbs. of him reflected that anger when I told him I needed his supplier's contact name and number.

"Damn it, I told you to leave it alone. Don't open that can of worms!"

And then I, who stood a foot shorter and was half his weight, snapped back, "I'm not opening the can of worms, I'm closing it!" Greg stood and glared, waiting for me to back down. I didn't. I explained that me calling the contact was the only way to resolve the non-conformance our project had been issued. Silence hung tensely between us, but I stood my ground, refusing to cave or avert my eyes. Finally, he broke his stance and strode over to his desk, muttering obscenities. He scribbled the supplier's name and number on a piece of paper and flung it at me, telling me I was "Dead wrong!" to be doing what I was doing. He knew that me getting involved to solve the issue would take away some of his authority, and he clearly didn't like that.

Greg, if you haven't already guessed, is a problem person, and he treated everyone in the office with equal disdain. I'd been on the project for about six weeks and had seen him bully, berate and belittle everyone he came into contact with. People had come to expect this behavior from him and, by not challenging it, sent the message that it was okay. But today, I snapped back.

The following days and weeks were difficult, to be sure. Greg made it a point to disregard and ignore me whenever possible (a challenge given that our desks were adjacent to one another). I didn't want any further confrontations, so I played along and ignored him at every turn.

After about a month of this, I realized how miserable I was going into the office. This game-playing had drained my energy and made me anxious. My guard was constantly up, and part of my energy always devoted to this negative interaction with Greg. So I decided I would do something completely illogical: I would inject energy into an otherwise dead work relationship.

Starting the following day, I would say "Good morning, Greg!" when I walked into the office, and wished him a good evening or weekend when I left. At first, he said nothing, then, he started to murmur or mumble something back in response. Eventually, he would respond to my greetings pleasantly. As the weeks progressed and I stayed this new course, our interactions became easier, smoother and more positive.

My decision to change the dynamic was rooted in a determination to treat him with the respect his position deserved. I'd always treated people well in the workplace, and this had led to energized, supportive and positive relationships. I decided that this relationship should be no different. I also became very clear on my own boundaries – knowing (and conveying) the line of disrespect that I wouldn't allow him to cross.

My strategy worked. Greg continued to treat me better than others in the office. He toned down his usual style with co-workers when I happened to be around, and generally acted in a more civil way.

Greg may have been especially difficult, but all people – even difficult people – need to know that they are respected and that disagreement or debate with them is about an issue, not them as a person. Once mutual respect is established, communications are always smoother.

I worked with Greg for over two years and he never raised his voice to me again. Every time it seemed that he was going to bark at me, I would let him know where he was going and that I didn't want it. I would like to say that Greg's behavior and demeanor changed on the whole, but that didn't happen. He continued to be the sort of person he always was with others, he only changed his ways for me. Imagine the change that could have happened if everyone worked with him the way I did.

Difficult people come in all forms and types with all sorts of difficulties but at the core, what all people want and need is respect for who they are. Once they know they are respected, they see conflicts differently – as being about issues and not people. The secret is to be hard on the issues, soft on the people. It's a matter of turning negative energy into positive energy.

LESSONS LEARNED

Greg is an extreme case of a problem person in the work place. To successfully shift my relationship with him, I applied the following lessons I've learned throughout my career on how to communicate with problem people:

Setting boundaries improves relationships

I decided early on that I would not tolerate someone yelling at me, nor would I allow being verbally or physically bullied. I always stand firm on being treated with respect and professionalism in the workplace. This doesn't mean that I need to be best friends with that difficult person, or that we need to even like each other's personalities, but mutual respect is key.

At the beginning of my engineering career, I was often the only woman in the workplace, so I encountered my share of unwelcoming (if not openly hostile) attitudes, words and situations. My job, however, required that I get things done even when people wanted to reject my input. I learned to use boundaries to help create respectful frameworks for discussions that would ensure respect for all parties, solve to the work problem at hand, and continue to build a work relationship that energized, rather than drained, the relationship.

Pause before hitting "Send"

We've all heard or experienced the wisdom of not hitting "send" on an email that we've written while angry. The advice goes: Write the message, save it and step away for a while.

One day, I found myself in that exact situation. A supplier had sent me a letter saying they weren't going to meet one of the terms of our agreement. I wrote a scathing email response about what would happen if they didn't honor our contract. I was furious because I had been working to give them more business (unbeknownst to them) but they weren't going to hold up their end of the deal. I hit save and had a co-worker read the email. He looked over the email and offered suggestions on how I could make my point without all the harsh words and outraged tone (and without possibly burning the bridge we'd built with this supplier). He was right, so I took some time to work on another task and calm down, then came back to the email. I ended up scrapping the original email, and writing a much better one that eventually resulted in them changing their stance and honoring our agreement. We went on to have a mutually beneficial relationship.

Just like with putting heated, reactive emails on "pause," taking time out from heated conversations or situations at work can save energy and unnecessary damage. When we're mad, we usually don't think clearly and have a hard time hearing the other person's perspective or position. In the heat of the moment, our brain triggers the "fight or flight" response, so we need to take time to calm down and deal rationally with the situation at hand.

Come from a place of respect

Take time to see the other's side. Few people like admitting they made a mistake, and problem people are even less likely to do so. In the case of Greg, he rarely admitted that he was wrong, and never ever did so publicly. I had to get the information I needed while allowing him to save face. This required some creativity, and a continued effort to treat him with respect. It was tempting to call him out for delaying a process unnecessarily, but doing so would have eroded the progress we'd made in changing our dynamic.

In another work situation a few years earlier, I was part of a department meeting where a co-worker inappropriately criticized me in front of about 40 other members of the department. She resented a protocol change I'd implemented to address safety concerns. While the change I had made wasn't popular, no one else reacted so disrespectfully or unprofessionally. I refused to get into an argument with her, but did listen to her perspective. I ended the discussion as politely as I could. Several of her co-workers apologized to me for her behavior, saying she was out of line. About a month later, this co-worker approached me to express her regrets for how she handled the situation and asked me to forgive her. She also shared her appreciation of the fact that I hadn't responded in kind to her. Because I had not responded angrily or disrespectfully to her, she was able to retain some of her dignity and she could recover gracefully from her error. I acknowledged that I had handled introducing the system change poorly and that I should have been more sensitive to the impact it would have on everyone. This conversation marked a shift in our interpersonal dynamic, and we ended up with a better working relationship and she became a great ally in the department.

KEY QUESTIONS

- How do you want people to treat you?

- Are you communicating with people in way that is consistent with your values?

- What can you do to change your communications to help ensure people treat you as you wish to be treated?

ACTION STEPS

When dealing with problem people it's important to keep your cool, know your limits and come from a place of mutual respect. This can be hard to do with particularly difficult people. It's important to develop strategies in advance to handle these kinds of situations.

1. Understand your triggers

Think of past situations that got you upset, angry or otherwise emotional. Take note of how the other person, or persons, acted, and how you responded when triggered.

2. Develop coping strategies

When you understand how you react in trigger situations, you can look at the possibilities for changing your response. Maybe that means walking away and coming back after everyone has had a chance to cool down. You could also get input from a neutral person, thereby seeing the situation from a different perspective. Developing a strong sense of your boundaries is also important.

3. Treat others well

All people respond to being treated with respect. If you want to be respected, be sure to show respect for everyone else. Remember to quickly admit if you made a mistake – this goes a long way in making the other person feel valued and "seen."

Whenever you can, give people a chance to save face.

By: Carol Dougherty

www.delta-group-llc.com

"Energize your workplace by showing respect for everyone. #EnergizedLeaders"

8: Serve to Lead, Lead to Serve

"I don't belong here."

The words on the page surprised me. What was so strange was that I was the one who had written them. I didn't remember feeling that way.

It had been several years since I had participated in the leadership course where I wrote those words. I was going back through my notes from the twelve weekly sessions, and thinking about how the course had opened my mind and heart to what leadership is really about. My understanding of leadership when I started the course was worlds away from my understanding now. At the beginning of the series we did a self-assessment. Describing my view of myself I had written those four words, so foreign now.

The course took place where I work, and I knew at least a little about each of the other eleven participants. As I looked at them it seemed to me they had it together. They were advancing boldly down their chosen career paths. I, on the other hand, had long since fallen off my career path and had landed in a . . . job. I saw myself as being so different from them – the black sheep in the fish pond, the square peg in the rhubarb pie.

But I was determined to make the most of my work situation and so I had decided to take the course in hopes of improving what little contribution I saw myself as having to offer in the corporate environment. I thought I needed it more than they needed me. Again: "I don't belong here."

In retrospect, now sitting and looking at those words (in my own handwriting), I see that I was holding up an ideal of what a leader looked like. I had created my perception of the mold that one needed to fit into in order to lead, and I'd thought it looked a lot like others but not me. And so, I didn't trust myself enough to let others trust me.

In those twelve weeks I learned good leadership tools and skills. But far more important than learning what I needed to do, I learned who I needed to *be*. Turns out, who I needed to be was me. Through the experience I came to see that my uniqueness was not that unique, that each of us had our own story of strengths and weaknesses, hopes and disappointments, celebrations and frustrations. There are commonalities that we all share that serve as points of potential connection. And I learned that for each of us, our uniqueness is not a weakness but rather a strength.

There was no mold of success that I needed to fit into. I didn't need to waste my energy trying to measure up to perceived expectations. There was no requirement for me to be something or someone I was not. I did need to grow, but first accepting myself as I am freed me from limiting beliefs and allowed that process to begin. I could trust myself just as I was, and so was worthy of trust from others. What I had to offer was precisely what the world needed, and that was me.

Though my life was changed in those twelve weeks, it was just the beginning of a new journey of learning, discovering and experiencing what it means to be a leader. In the course, I learned that trust is the foundation of leadership and with every step of my journey I gain a deeper understanding of how true that is.

Trust is the link that connects service to leadership. In service we build trust. In trust we build leadership. All this happens in relationship, person to person – together. Every person has their own unique contribution to offer the world, their own skills, their knowledge, their perspectives, their story. Whenever anyone withholds their unique contribution, it leaves a void that nobody else can fill. But when we share of ourselves to the benefit of all, this is service. This is where the path to leadership begins.

LESSONS LEARNED

Wherever you are, you belong there because where you are is where you need to begin. When climbing a mountain, basecamp isn't established on the summit – it's established at the base. And leadership doesn't begin on the high plateau of lofty ideals. It starts with really understanding who you are, what your needs are and what you have to offer. When in service, you are open to share and to receive the connections that ultimately provide our greatest source of personal energy.

Be a servant first

Service is being before doing. In order for you to make your unique contribution, you need to know who you are and understand what it is that makes you unique. Then you can live that out in what you do, serving in action shaped by a primary concern for the welfare of the individual, including both others *and* self. The point of servant leadership is not what I do but what WE become.

Service is others before self. But it's not about others *instead* of self. Service is about giving of yourself without giving up yourself. Exhaustion is not a mark of success or badge of honor. No one becomes more from another becoming less. When each gives, all grow.

Service is compassion embodied – it shows others we have their best interest at heart. Service is more than helping others (helping others can actually be a disservice if we're not careful). When others actualize more of their potential as a result of our actions, then we are serving.

Service is about going deeper before going farther. Servant leadership isn't a leader going the extra mile to do something nice for others. It's a servant going deeper to be someone of significance to others.

Service creates trust

When we are living our lives in service, making our unique contribution for the benefit of all, then there is fertile soil for the seeds of trust to grow. In service, you are revealing your true, authentic self, and authenticity is always the first step in building trust. In order for others to trust you, they need to know who you are.

Authentic actions reveal a trustworthy soul that others may then choose to trust. We don't "earn" trust, as much as build it through relationship. Trust is not a commodity. We rely on people for the results they produce. We have confidence in their abilities. But we *trust* them for who they are. If you trust them simply for what you need them to do for you, you will be disappointed. They will make mistakes, they will let you down, they may even betray you. But trust is always in the person, and has within it an element of grace.

Service creates connections that trust weaves into relationships and communities. It gathers people around a common purpose to write a shared story. Relationship shows us what it is that makes us unique. If I see an area that is a weakness for me but is a strength for you, I can then allow and encourage you to make your unique contribution in that area. And you in turn will then trust me to make my contribution in areas where I am strong.

Trust grows leadership

Lives of service bound by trust provide a solid foundation for leadership. Leadership doesn't begin with a promotion or an appointment – it begins with a choice. Being a leader begins when you choose to make a difference in and through the lives of others. Leadership begins when others choose to follow. That choice to follow is based on trust. Robert Greenleaf, who coined the term servant leadership, said people will "freely respond only to individuals who are chosen as leaders because they are proven and trusted as servants."

Trust paves the way for change. A trusted leader asks people to move from the familiar to the unfamiliar. Only with trust will people allow their day-to-day decisions and actions to be guided by a new vision. People will choose to follow a trusted servant who has demonstrated compassion for who they are and a passion for who they can become.

When a servant is trusted, he or she sets an example for others to model in their own service. Mutual service builds trust within the community and brings its members closer together. And when the trusted servant is chosen as a leader, it sets an expectation for others to also choose to be leaders, further strengthening the community and broadening its influence. From service – leadership. From leadership – service.

KEY QUESTIONS

- **Serve**: In each role in your life how are you giving of yourself to the benefit of all?

- **Trust**: In what ways can you strengthen the trust you have in others and others have in you?

- **Lead**: Do you see your leadership as a way of serving?

ACTION STEPS

1. Reflect

Think about your own story to better understand what you have to offer. The more you know about who you are, the better you can align your actions in authentic service. Listen to the stories of others to better understand their needs. Serve. Build trust. Be trustworthy.

2. Let Go

Trust, and let go. Let go, like I had to, of false expectations and misperceptions of leadership. Trust yourself for who you are, as you are. Whatever your role, whether it's in an organization or not, whether it's in management or not, see that role as an opportunity to serve, to build trust, and to lead.

Let go of the fear of your own brilliance. You weren't made to fit in. You *are* made to stand out in all your unique splendor. We are all unique. Imagine what might come to be if everyone lived into their unique purpose. Fitting in only leads to mediocrity. Coming together as who we are produces an exponentially greater collective energy.

3. **Connect**

Identify your key relationships, the ones you have and those you should but don't. Identify ways you can get to know each other better in order to deepen connection and strengthen the trust you share.

Trust others. Let go of your need for control. "Control is the antithesis of trust," says Michael Ayers. Leadership has never been about control and never will be. In a world of immense uncertainty and chaos, leadership influences people to grow into the fullness of who they are meant to be.

At the very center of the word trust is "us." Life is a grand messy thing and we're in it together. In relationships formed by service and bound by trust we will discover the energy to ignite life and our leadership will break through the mess to a world that is grander still.

By Daniel Buhr
www.Cybuhr.com
"In service we build trust. In trust we build leadership. #EnergizedLeaders"

ENERGIZE

YOUR
WORKPLACE

Energize Your Workplace

An organization, like any collective of people, is not just the sum of its individuals but an entity unto itself. Together, these collected people form a singular organism with its own behavior and culture. We hope for one whose energy crackles with positivity and growth. Although *all* the insights in this book can be applied at the organization level, in this part we look at four factors that are especially crucial to an organization's collective energy reserves:

1. Brand "You":

All organizations are also brands and brands generate great energy but authentic brands need to have a solid foundation. The foundations of authentic brands are found in the people who support those brands and the individuals who see their personal brand as being synchronous with the organization's brand.

2. Gut Thinking:

Leaders often have to disregard the various facts in front of them and instead "lead from the gut." When candid and open communications and actions are encouraged throughout the workplace, the result is an empowered and energized workforce that is encouraged to rely on its intuition and gut feeling.

3. Gratitude-Based Organizational Attitude:

Gratitude is often only reserved for major events or achievements, and limits its influence on our everyday life. Creating a culture of gratitude in all areas assures greater recognition and appreciation across all levels of an organization, resulting in higher engagement and energy.

4. Love Multiplies:

A workplace culture based on love is a beautiful concept, but that again begins with a leader who demonstrates and appreciates the nature of love and also loves him or herself. Once a leader can do this, it is simply a matter of introducing a culture of love into the organization and allow it to flourish and reproduce.

9: Brand You, Brand Your Organization

I was diagnosed with juvenile diabetes at the age of 8. I gradually learned what it means to live as a diabetic, from adapting my diet to self-injecting insulin doses daily. You could say I had a head start in resiliency-building, learning along the way that I did not have to let the process of managing my health keep me from my pursuing my dreams and goals. With my family's support, and my own determination and adaptability, I have successfully managed my condition ever since. I am strong, independent and face the challenges that life offers me with an openness that I've learned to cultivate over time.

When it came time to decide on a career, I gravitated towards those vocations that would allow me to help people. My first choice (medical doctor) was not an option because of a wariness on the part of medical colleges in admitting students with medical conditions. So my doctor and my parents advised me to achieve my vision of helping people through a different path.

I chose a faculty in Business and Commerce. After graduation, I became a chartered accountant and began living my new dream of joining an International Bank. My trademark resilience and drive came into play despite my fears about the aggressive nature of the investment world. Every day, I learned new skills and took on new challenges. I adapted my style, grew out of my shyness and became assertive without being aggressive. I thrived and excelled in a male-dominated industry, positively impacted the ROI of my clients and grew a loyal client base.

I didn't realize it at the time, but I was building a personal brand of courage, drive and determination to get things done. In one word: Resilience.

Years later, a conversation with a friend prompted me to revisit my brand – specifically, what did my brand *mean*? What did I want it to represent? Yes, I was resilient – it was who I was at the core, but how was it manifesting itself more widely than simply as a reactive stance? In other words, how was I to take my personal brand and actually be proactive in *doing* something with it instead of just pulling it out when confronted with challenges?

This was when I realized that I wanted to use my brand to help others recognize theirs. This was my "aha" moment – where I reconnected with my purpose, inner drive and vision of helping people. I wanted to build an organization and a life where not only I was resilient, but the organization itself was based on the concept of resilience. So I quit the corporate world and set up my company. By becoming an executive coach and trainer, I reinvented myself and translated my vision into one that could help people on their own journeys of growth and development.

As with any deep and worthwhile journey, there are still challenges and setbacks along the way. Just a short time ago, I was having coffee with new friends, and I was introduced to the group as an ex-investment banker. One of the women asked what I did now, and I froze. In that moment of seemingly-endless silence, my mind raced, asking "Who Am I? What am I doing? How do I explain how I moved from finance to executive coaching?"

I've had to remember to be patient and kind to myself. I am still living – and creating – this transition from an investment banker to an executive coach and trainer. When I look at the transition, I see that I've made it a success by training and coaching myself, practicing relentlessly and living many aspects of my life out of my comfort zone.

I am a client value creator on the human side – I love to motivate, inspire and support people's positive potential. Discovering and articulating the value my clients bring to the world is what drives what I do, and is a key aspect of my personal vision. Helping my clients in this way brings me a joy that I never found in the investment world.

My resilience, persistence, willingness to take risks in life and follow my vision with not only passion but patience and endurance have given me invaluable insights to energized leadership. If you lead by example, you influence those lives you touch positively. Living an intentional life is being present in all that you do and consciously taking steps to achieve your vision or purpose in life. You demonstrate leadership in who you are, by your character and your credibility.

Inspired leadership also means increased energy – for everyone. You can revitalize yourself by the energy you bring to what you do and in the way you articulate your purpose. The people whose lives you touch will be energized when you inspire them to find their purpose.

Reconnecting with my vision has not only helped me steer through difficulties and challenges, but has helped me define myself and my brand, and develop the resilience to joyfully embrace this journey called "My Life."

LESSONS LEARNED

My values and vision have shaped who I am and what I do, and have guided me through my corporate career of 20 years and into my current journey as a coach and trainer. Here are some things I've learned along the way.

Believing in myself helped me succeed

Some of my most important lessons came from my fears and adversities. My experiences enabled me to stop underestimating my talents and abilities and to ignore unproductive fears.

Don't give credence to your doubts or buy into the idea that you're not meant to do what you want to do or that you're not capable of doing it. If you listen to your fears, you will not reach your full potential. Believe in yourself and your purpose.

Identifying my vision energized my brand

Identifying my vision has helped me to find answers to questions such as "What do I want to be?," 'What do I want to stand for?," "Does my work matter?," and "How do I differ in what I do?"

You help your clients, your business, and your organization by aligning the internal truths with the external brand so you can differentiate yourself in what you do.

Aligning with your vision lets you to focus your attention on what matters most, what you want to accomplish in life, and most of all what kind of human being you are in the way you influence those around you. It is something that enables you to act and make constructive changes towards a future you want to see. A purpose-driven vision breathes life into who you are and is the fuel of sustained life and leadership. Without a vision or an end in mind you are like an aimless wanderer.

Visions evolve

During my 20 years in that male-dominated work environment, I reinvented myself several times and I made a significant change by becoming an entrepreneur. Why? I realized that I wanted to wake up every morning and feel awake – to help people become more effective leaders, create transformational change personally and professionally, and embrace and foster accountability.

The key is to focus on your achievements and successes in times of challenge, and to learn from your setbacks. If you connect all those things back to your inner purpose, you can't help but stay true to your vision. You may even see that your vision changes over time – and that's fine, as long as it's aligned with your values and purpose.

KEY QUESTIONS

How do you become a force for your own life? Ask three key questions of yourself:

- Why am I here and where am I headed?

- How am I going to get there?

- What legacy am I going to leave?

ACTION STEPS

1.   **Identify your vision**

I see a personal vision as a chart that's plotted in a way that it is rooted in your past, deals with your present and sets the tone for your future. Your vision is the longer view and the elevator of your leadership. It provides the underlying foundation for creating a brand that resonates with your core self and connects with others. It's your purpose in life, the thing that gives you deep joy and answers the question "Why am I here?"

2.   Look 10 years into the future

Write down what your vision is for 10 years from now. This can act as a grounding force, help remind you of your core identity in moments of adversity and transitions. Once you have the 10 year picture ahead of you, it's time to think about your strategy. What will you accomplish in your personal life and career in the next year that will be a stepping stone to the final vision.

After identifying your vision, and acknowledging that you have the intent to move towards it, then the next step is action. Create a strategy of action steps that will lead towards your 10 year vision. It may help to look at who you can collaborate with to achieve your vision, and assess the talents and skills you'll need along the way.

3.   Find your three P's

Once you're clear on your vision, you can translate it into your personal brand. There are three Ps to building your brand: your Promise, your Positioning and your Personality.

Your **Promise** is what you stand for. It's what you offer and want to deliver to your clients. It represents by your character, your integrity, and your core values.

Your **Positioning** is how you differentiate yourself and add value in achieving the promise you have made to your clients, colleagues, work environment and anyone else whose life you influence.

Your **Personality** is the platform you use to share your brand perspective. You are your personal brand and walk and talk your reputation.

A personal brand that identifies who you are at the core is essential to finding what you really want in life and work. And as a leader, a personal brand can also translate into an organizational brand that taps into the leader's energy and multiplies and amplifies his or her personal brand top the benefit of all.

By Lalita Raman

www.transitionsintl.com

"You can revitalize yourself by the energy you bring to what you do and in the way you articulate your purpose. #EnergizedLeaders"

10: Encourage "Gut Thinking"

I am naturally hard-wired to listen to my heart. Ever since I was a little girl, the needs of others have driven most of my decisions. In my academic and career tracks, I learned to leverage more of my brain, to review data and approach things more logically.

But absolutely none of my natural wiring or my training emphasized the importance of listening to my gut when weighing critical decisions. It wasn't until I was in a particularly difficult life phase that I discovered the power that lies in our gut.

I was in the midst of the most challenging time in my life. It was a three-year stretch (that seemed like an eternity) where my husband and I were faced with one stress-filled situation after another. The first turned our lives upside down and the others just kept upping the odds that we wouldn't return to "normal" life anytime soon.

We were about halfway through the three years, with no end in sight. I was living in Louisiana in a fairly new job and a new lease. He was living in Tulsa, and had a new job that required constant travel all across the U.S. Our home was in Houston, sitting dormant on the market amid a crashing economy.

The pain that lingered from the situation that started it all was still consuming my waking thoughts and causing fitful nights. The reality of daily life without my partner added another layer of constant pressure: I didn't have my husband to wake up and come home to, and we had no idea how long we'd have to endure separation.

One afternoon as I was feeling especially vulnerable I remembered a passage in the Bible that talked about the Armor of God (armor sounded like exactly what I needed to keep functioning). I am a visual learner, so I grabbed my pencil, opened that source of wisdom and prepared to draw each piece of armor, hoping to plant a mental picture that really resonated.

And then I read the first line: "Stand firm then, with the belt of truth buckled around your waist."

"What?" I said, dropping the pencil. "Why is truth a *belt*? Shouldn't truth be in your brain and protected by your helmet, or in your heart and protected by the breastplate? Or even in your shoes like a firm foundation? Why would a belt be labeled something as important as 'truth'?"

And then like a bolt of lightning, an image flashed through my mind: Someone was being told a very painful truth, and physically doubling over in extreme pain.

"Interesting," I thought, "What if truth is first discerned in our gut?"

And then a powerful memory flooded my brain. It was the very first time my gut told me something was wrong . . . really wrong. I was a teenager at a summer camp, and each time I came in contact with a particular counselor, my gut kicked. And each time, my brain argued with my gut, telling it that I had an overactive imagination, that I was acting childish, that there was no way a counselor at a Christian camp could act inappropriately. And each time I believed my brain over my gut, my stomach would churn more intensely.

Even though I did not embrace right away what my gut was telling me, I stayed safe because I eventually did. I'm just glad I listened in time, because my gut was right all along.

That memory was followed by an explosion of other memories that all pointed to the truth that our gut just knows.

I remembered the time that I started a new job, and learned something about one of my new employee's work preferences in a one-on-one meeting. I later shared that information with my boss (which, in hindsight, was my first mistake) and he encouraged me to include it in her review.

My gut kicked, but I did what I was advised to do instead of listening to my gut.

That decision destroyed all the trust that employee had in me, and scared the team I had just been hired to serve. She left for another opportunity soon after, and it took several very long months for me to regain the trust of the rest of the team. I had to prove to them, beyond a doubt, that I had made one very bad decision and that I had no intention of repeating it.

That memory opened the door to others where my gut was right about hiring decisions.

In one case, a peer had been promoted and we were trying to fill his position so he could move to his new role. We'd interviewed several people, none of whom seemed to fit and all of whom we passed on. Pretty soon, enough time had passed that our promoted peer was getting impatient at being held back by his old job. His impatience reached its limit just as we were interviewing a candidate that my gut knew would be a bad fit.

Everyone felt the pressure to say yes to the candidate, so they did. My gut said he would operate with a "my way or the highway" style and that it would be harmful to the team. So I said no. Pressure gave way, and the candidate was hired.

His first day on the job, I received voicemail and email messages from my teammates. They had just come from a meeting with the new hire and were reaching out to apologize for not listening to my "gut instinct."

In another case, my gut didn't just *kick in* during the interview—it *churned*. I was absolutely convinced the candidate sitting across from me was lying. I let my team members know. Like before, it was a race against time, and the candidate was hired in a hurry. Nearly two years later, I received a phone call from an exhausted leader who was dealing with a situation bigger than Pandora's box. He said, "I should have listened to you."

Then I remembered the time I was asked to help to put together an expert panel for a Chamber of Commerce event in another city. Towards the end of our planning, we were given a script for introducing our panel.

Immediately my gut responded, reminding me that my gift is to be in the crowd, engaging them where they are, and making sure that everyone is a part of the process. Standing behind a podium and adopting a formal stance could create a barrier with the audience and keep me from leveraging my gift.

However, I understood that the event coordinators' goal was to keep the event and speakers on schedule. And even though I knew I could stick to the schedule, I wanted to be supportive of the Chamber staff's work, so I said nothing.

As I stood at the podium several weeks later, I looked out at the attendees and knew immediately that my gut had been right. If I had listened to it, I'd be interacting with them in a very different format, serving them in alignment with my natural gifts.

LESSONS LEARNED

My gut had been speaking truth to me for years

Before my heart felt it and before the data was there, there were alarms about physical danger, cues on how to be a better leader, warnings about bad hiring decisions, and nudges on how to leverage my gifts to serve others at a higher level.

That belt of truth is the first piece of armor listed, making it very significant. Its job is to wrap around our mid-section and protect those gut instincts. Remember that your gut may tell you something that does not seem to make logical sense. There may be no data to back it up. But when you learn to decipher it, you can rely on it for truth.

The more I tune into my gut, the louder it speaks

My gut has helped me learn to avoid energy

leaks by pushing me to speak up when I haven't been, urging me to be quiet when I've been over-sharing, helping me identify potential landmines with business alliances, and encouraging me to either trust people or be cautious.

Most people recognize the power in their guts subconsciously. Whether they follow it or not is another story. Recently, I polled my social media circle on whether they had ever regretted not listening to their gut. An incredible 100% said yes.

I don't believe that our gut should be our only guide

We were all given a brain, a heart and a gut for a reason. If we are only leveraging one or two of those, we are working the rest of them harder. When we learn to tap into all three, we bring our greatest wisdom, our greatest strength, our greatest energy and our greatest endurance to whatever situation or task we face.

I've also learned that the ONLY time my gut has been wrong is when my fear has been disguised as intuition. Truth is not Fear. Fear is generated in your mind. It's about comfort, past pain, ego, the need to be right or your preconceived notions. Wisdom serves others without sacrificing your values.

KEY QUESTIONS

- Have you ever regretted not listening to your gut?

- What are all the factors that drive your decisions?

- How would learning to tune into your gut increase your energy and fuel your leadership?

ACTION STEPS

Today my husband and I are back under the same roof, living in a part of the world we once said that we would never live in. And we are here because we followed the process below, and tapped into our whole-selves. Making the decision to live here was way outside of our comfort zone. But the adventure, the learning, the friendships, the travel, and the growth we are experiencing continue to evidence that our guts were right.

Finding the energy you need is just like drilling for oil. It is one thing to know where it lies. It is another thing to learn how to access it. Here are some things you can do to access your "black gold":

1. Pray and meditate about it.

2. Pause; turn on some music and journal.

3. Evaluate what's driving you. Is it fear or wisdom?

By: Chery Gegelman

www.consultgiana.com

"What if truth is first discerned in our gut? #EnergizedLeaders"

11: Build an Organization of Gratitude

My childhood was not exactly typical. As a result, the circumstances of my early formative years instilled in me the practice of never taking anything for granted and of trying to appreciate every little thing in life.

I was 11 years old when the civil war started in Lebanon, my home country. At that time, my country was under siege; ports and airports were partially operational which disrupted the import of several goods and raw materials from abroad such as wheat and crude oil. This meant a shortage of bread and gas in the country, and people lined up in front of bakeries and gas stations to make their most basic purchases. This, in turn, made such locations *strategic* targets for shelling and explosions.

An incident that I can never forget happened when I came home from school one day to find it empty. Mum was always at home when I got back from school, so I thought she might be visiting some neighbors or shopping in a local store. I went to my room to study while waiting for Mum, Dad and my sisters and brothers to come home from their respective universities and workplaces.

For our daily supply of bread, Dad and my older brother alternated going to the bakery after coming back from work. They and many others waited in the long queues to buy the bread. One or the other would typically be at the bakery around 4:30 p.m. and reach home 30 minutes later.

On that day around 4:30 p.m., a huge explosion tore through our neighborhood. As smoke and flames filled the streets, the radio announced that the explosions had taken place at a nearby bakery.

At that moment, all I could think of was that either my dad or my brother had been caught in the explosion. I broke down in tears, not knowing what to do or who to contact. At that time, of course, there were no cell phones and regular landlines quickly got blocked in such situations. I was totally in despair until one of our neighbors knocked at the door to check if any of us had gone to the bakery. She found me crying and tried to comfort me, but comfort would only come from knowing that my father and brother were safe. Then she left to see if any of the neighbors knew where my mum was and came back with some good news: Mum and Dad had left unexpectedly to attend the funeral of a distant relative. Dad could not have been at the bakery, so I knew he was safe. Shortly thereafter, my brother arrived home highly distressed: He was worried about Dad, as it was his turn to buy the bread that day. Everyone arrived later than usual that day because they were trapped in the traffic jam that resulted from the explosion.

That evening, we were all quiet at dinner and grateful for our old relative who by his natural death saved us from a tragedy! Seeing all of us at the table that evening was a real blessing and filled my heart with gratitude. I definitely did not take my life or that of anyone else for granted, bearing in mind that about 100 people were killed and injured as a result of that explosion.

Incidents like these continued happening over the period of the civil war. Several times, my family members and I barely managed to escape injury and even death. We experienced all sorts of violence—shelling, bomb explosions, shootings, fighting and attempted kidnapping. The thing I recall most is the deep silence that we regrouped in after every close call: a silence that resulted from the feeling of shock, disbelief and deep gratitude that we were still alive and unharmed.

Looking back on those 15 long years living in a war zone, I see that growing up in such circumstances deeply affected me, shaped my very personality, and taught me how to break through difficulties by appreciating life's most basic gifts: being alive, being in good health and being surrounded by family and friends.

LESSONS LEARNED

There's truth in the saying that we appreciate the light only after having been in the darkness. My own experiences, trying as they were, taught me some valuable lessons.

Remember what a precious privilege it is to be alive

When the explosion destroyed the bakery, my father and brother could have been hurt, if not killed. But God's grace saved their lives on that day. Numerous times during nights of heavy shelling, I did not expect to see the dawn and yet I did! Fierce storms always calm down, and resilient ships continue their journeys.

Our blessings are always within us and within our reach. The ability to breathe, love and work is our greatest blessing. If we consider how many people worldwide are suffering from poverty, violence and wars, then the mere fact of having a normal, peaceful life becomes a blessing in itself. Furthermore, we should never worry about any material loss, as homes and businesses can be rebuilt but human loss is permanent.

Don't let fear poison your life and attitude

During the civil war, I learned to overcome my fears by remembering the many times I had survived and by letting fear pass through me quickly. After every nightmarish experience, I tried to find reasons to be grateful, to take some lessons from the mess and to find the motivation to work harder and achieve more. In the back of my mind, there was always the thought that I might not have another chance to repeat what I was doing so I better do it well the first time around.

Forget yesterday – all you have is today

If I had obsessed about what happened in that explosion or any other act of violence I survived during the war, I would have never been able to do anything with my life. Did I collapse and feel sorry for myself? No. On the contrary, I made sure to take advantage of every moment I was alive and every source of energy I had within me.

My family's reunion at the dinner table the evening of the explosion highlighted the importance of being together as a family. I saw the importance of always appreciating the presence of family and friends in life. As we surround ourselves with people we love, we can overcome fear and feel stronger. The support of parents, siblings, friends and neighbors can make all the difference.

We don't all live in a country torn by civil war, but we are all living through some kind of a war. Keeping a grateful attitude makes us see the positive in every situation — even those that are ugly and violent. It also gives us the drive and energy to get up, shake off the dust, rebuild what was broken and move on with our lives.

KEY QUESTIONS

A grateful mindset enables you to overcome the stress of your current situation and lets you shine the light in the midst of your darkness and despair.

- What are the positive aspects in your life, and how can you emphasize them in order to enhance your happiness?

- When was the last time you showed appreciation and gratitude to your colleagues, friends and family?

- What are the negative thoughts that are pulling you down, and how can your reverse them in order to energize your leadership?

ACTION STEPS

Try to remain positive even in the midst of difficult circumstances. Focusing on your loss and getting depressed will not solve any of your problems. It will only prevent you from seeing possible solutions and putting them into effect.

1. Be happy with who you are and what you do

Take a moment to remember those who are less fortunate than you and be grateful for what you have. In this way, your fear of losing vanishes and abundance is yours.

Remember that every day we receive enough to be thankful for. By being grateful, we become less focused on that which we're trying to acquire, which gives us more patience and self-control over our emotions and impulses. In this way, gratitude can become a tool of self-soothing and comfort.

2. Acknowledge and appreciate

Cultivate the habit of being grateful for every good thing that comes to you and everyone who has helped you. Show your appreciation and give thanks to all who have helped you and made a difference in your life.

Be a role model for leading with gratitude and let your heart lead the way. Those you lead will be inspired to learn from your example. They will cultivate similar attitudes and behaviors.

Life in Lebanon remains far from perfect today, and acts of violence still erupt occasionally and unexpectedly. Sometimes I feel exhausted thinking about it. But when I focus on my family and on what I've managed to achieve in my education and career, my heart is filled with gratitude and I feel energized. You too can energize your leadership by taking steps to manifest your gratitude.

3. Simplify rather than overanalyze

Think of a few phrases relevant to any situation that's causing you stress or pain. Highlight the negative feelings that might come out from each phrase, and instead of assuming these negative feelings to be the possible outcomes try, on the other hand, to appreciate the consequences of the opposite positive aspects of the situation. Compare these positive aspects to other positive attitudes you took before and which you were grateful to.

By: Hoda Maalouf

www.HodaMaalouf.com

"Be grateful for what you have. Your fear of losing vanishes, and abundance is yours. #EnergizedLeaders"

12: Love and Let Love Multiply

My relationship with love did not begin well. I learned early in life to guard my heart and to meet any act of "love" with suspicion. This even included any attempt at self-love. Yet I hoped that if I was good enough or successful enough, I could somehow earn that which I so desperately craved. I believed love was something that comes from outside-in rather than inside-out.

I experienced criticism as rejection and quickly turned the negativity inward, reinforcing the belief that somehow I was unlovable. I refused to accept praise, instead choosing to embrace unworthiness while pretending to be humble. As a leader, I developed the shameful habit of seeking to win approval through manipulation rather than earning respect by focusing on service, integrity and transparency. As a follower, I agreed to every request or demand on my time and attempted to control circumstances so as to never disappoint.

Looking back, I see that I was in a constant state of worry and exhaustion. My sleep was fitful, I gained weight and found unhealthy ways to medicate or distract my mind from all these negative emotions. My health suffered, my work suffered and my family suffered. I was always seeking love but was never satisfied, compelled to prove myself over and over again.

Eventually this way of living and leading became unsustainable. I was on a treadmill of overwork, coping, burnout, crash, recovery and back to overwork. This was all in an effort to earn the love I refused myself. Unwittingly, I'd set myself up for perpetual disappointment. In the process, I alienated the very people I desperately wanted to please. The suffering eventually became so painful, that I reached a point where I knew I had to swallow my pride and accept that I needed help.

On a balmy July evening, I rolled my motorcycle into the parking lot of a small catholic church across town to join a meeting that a friend had suggested. Seven or eight cars dotted the lot built for a hundred or more. I was early so I sat on my bike for several minutes staring anxiously at the church and debating a quick retreat. Eventually, I pushed aside the fear and willed my feet to take the first steps towards the church door and down the stairs to the basement.

The cinder block basement was painted a faded, avocado green and illuminated by exposed, florescent ceiling lights reminiscent of an old hospital or psychiatric ward. In the center of the room was a small stand with a few Styrofoam cups and a pot of coffee. Metal folding chairs were arranged in a circle and sitting in those chairs were men whom you would likely never find together in any other setting. The attire ranged from a buttoned down collar with loose tie to a Hawaiian shirt with an old baseball cap. It wasn't what I expected but in a way, comforting.

As I approached the circle a rather large man wearing a grease-stained, auto service uniform stood, offered a friendly handshake and directed me to the coffee. I had more than enough nervous energy but I figured the coffee cup would give me something to do with my hands. I sat down with my cup and the remaining men politely introduced themselves. The meeting started with little fanfare, just a brief overview of the purpose, agenda and rules for the group. With that, we were underway.

I barely recall the comments the other men made as we went around the circle sharing the lessons life had taught us during the previous week. I wasn't required to speak but I decided it would be ok to dip my toe in the water and say a few words. I was determined to carefully manage my comments, (a habit I'd established for maintaining emotional distance), but after about 10 minutes my protective barrier shattered and I blurted out my story in a torrent of tears, anguish and relief.

As I sat there, spent and ragged from my confession, I felt an arm around my shoulders and heard words of encouragement, empathy and understanding. No judgment, no questions, no advice, just the comforting presence of another human being who understood my suffering. Others began to speak, sharing pieces of their story and offering hope. I arrived looking for answers but what I found was love and acceptance. No performance required.

Over the months that followed I spent every Thursday night with this band of misfits learning how to forgive myself, love myself, love others and approach the world with a new perspective. We created a community that empowered us to change our stories and allowed us to free ourselves from attachment to external approval with the resulting symptoms of and low self-esteem and constant anxiety.

I learned that love changes everything. And that love starts with me.

Love is your deepest need and the source of your greatest acts of courage, compassion and commitment. Love supplies a wellspring of energy, belief and hope that can take you beyond what you thought was possible. Love can also push you far from your comfort zone leaving you vulnerable to rejection and pain. To lead from a heart full of love is an audacious journey but one that promises to give meaning and passion to your life and work.

LESSONS LEARNED

Through this journey I came to realize that the expectations I set for myself, and others, were unrealistic and would leave me trapped in a cycle of defeat. I now understood that my beliefs about love were based on a story I created in order to survive. I made the decision to seek a new way of being that would allow me to experience the freedom of love and leadership with an open heart.

Empathy for others requires empathy for self

I began by forgiving myself and finding new ways to appreciate my uniqueness and potential without the burden of guilt and shame. I would still set goals and strive to improve, but with a focus on progress and a willingness to be flexible and patient. When others complimented me or showed affection I began to incorporate these feelings into the view I held of myself. I recognized there was much good in who I was and who I could become. When faced with criticism, I refused to beat myself up or internalize the comments, choosing instead to learn what I could from the experience and move on.

Fear is the enemy of vulnerability

Instead of acting out of the fear of rejection, I developed the confidence to lead more authentically. I learned to share more of myself, become vulnerable, admit my mistakes and ask for help while maintaining my self-esteem and nurturing healthy interdependence. As I moved towards others they moved towards me, and their support became a source of much needed encouragement and energy.

I also learned the difference between love and approval. Approval is conditional and temporary. When we seek affirmation or approval, it satisfies us for only so long, until we need it again, (and the cycle continues). Love, on the other hand, is steady. I came to know that I was worthy of love, no matter what the external situation. In that strength I was able to focus on accomplishment through service to others rather than approval as a source of self-worth. I developed daily rituals and maintained a system of support outside of work that provided the energy to stay on course when the old beliefs emerged out of stress or in the face of a new challenge.

Love expands our influence

My coworkers sensed the change in me and responded. We built deeper, more personal connections. Communication and cooperation improved. Each new experience we shared reinforced the change and over time we learned how to support one another as individuals while in pursuit of a common goal. We were becoming a community that in some ways resembled the group that had helped me so much in my journey. There would be challenges along the way but we were committed to bringing our hearts into our work and building healthy relationships. We thrived in the new environment and as we added new team members we looked for people who would share our values.

KEY QUESTIONS

- How does the image you hold of yourself impact your leadership?

- Who have you invited into in your life to help you maintain a balanced perspective?

- What steps do you take to maintain a healthy level of self-love, boundaries and balance?

ACTION STEPS

How you view and treat yourself will profoundly influence how you approach your leadership and relate to those you lead. Maybe you've been operating on autopilot, unaware of why you act the way we do but painfully aware of the consequences.

The first step to any significant change is to make an honest assessment of your life and admit that you need to take action. Consider these basic steps to help you get started in your journey.

1. Assess your self-love

Pay attention to the language you use to describe yourself and how you see yourself in relation to others. Listen to both your internal and external dialogue. How do these judgments influence your behavior? How do they make you feel? Write it down. At the end of the week, read your notes and consider what they reveal about your self-perception. In the same notebook, write down the ways you think those views may impact your relationships and leadership and how you can begin to change your story.

2.   Seek out support

Set up a time to meet with someone you trust and who will speak with you truthfully. Ask them for their perspective on how you treat yourself and others. Talk about the way you maintain or don't maintain appropriate boundaries with others. Focus on listening without defensiveness. This is an opportunity to learn and gain insight into areas where you can change. Again, write down and reflect on the things you learn.

Find a group of like-minded people to meet with on a regular basis who will challenge and encourage you towards a healthy view of yourself, provide a loving community and encourage you to be honest and authentic.

3. Establish daily rituals

As you begin to make changes in your life there are daily rituals that can help you establish these new ways of thinking and being. Consider regular exercise and improving your diet. See this as an act of self-love designed to improve your energy and strengthen your body. Set aside time each morning to meditate or just have some quiet time with your thoughts before your day begins. You might reflect on teaching or reading that is directed toward the changes you want to make in your life. Set your intention towards how you want to be in the world today. Expressing your story in a journal can also be a powerful resource for change. Finally, when your head hits the pillow each night, spend a few minutes affirming the progress you are making, expressing gratitude for your life and remembering that you are worthy of love.

By: Scott Mabry

www.soul2work.com

"Leadership clarifies. Love Connects.
#EnergizedLeaders"

ENERGIZE

YOUR FUTURE

Energize Your Future

The future is often presented as some uncertain void of chaos and unpredictability, and while this is true to a large extent, such a representation also ignores the fact that we are each armed with those tools that can give us the best chance at success in the future. But how best to energize a future that holds so much unknown? Here are four concepts to do just that:

1. Have a Plan B:

Plan B's are often thought of as fallbacks and defaults but they can often be every bit as fulfilling, and surprisingly, sometimes even more so, than whatever Plan A was. The idea is always to have alternatives because the future is uncertain, but having options helps guard against potential fallouts and helps maintain the level of energy needed for ongoing success.

2. Recognize the Role of Fun:

Challenges are often best countered with fun. The fact remains that we are often constrained by our own thought patterns when we try and deal with a challenge, but old patterns can't win over new challenges. When you have fun with a challenge, you free up your neural pathways to explore different options and approaches. And let's face it, fun is energy.

3. Explore the Unknown:

Curiosity is the key to all learning, and learning is the key to the future. To be an expert in what is already known is nothing great, but to explore the unknown and to be curious about things that others may not see helps you to gain the advantage when it comes to having more knowledge and a wider understanding of any situation.

4. Face Whatever Comes with Positivity:

A positive outlook has never been a liability and will always serve anyone well in any scenario. Nothing is more energetic than positivity.

13: Plan (B) for the Future

For me, becoming an FBI agent was Plan B.

Growing up on a cattle ranch in the middle of Wyoming, I yearned for a life of excitement. I graduated with a Business Degree because I thought it would open doors in the world of fast-moving finance. It didn't take long for me to find the routine of an office job terribly boring—there was no adventure, no excitement, no real challenges to keep my mind alert and creative.

After a bit of research, I decided that the U.S. Foreign Service was the answer to my dilemma. Lots of travel to exotic lands and immersion in foreign cultures—it sounded like my dream job. I carefully ticked off all the requirements needed to apply, filled out a background form and sent off my application.

I waited for several weeks, enduring the office job, until the Foreign Service finally replied. They invited me to complete the next steps of the application process. My mind came alive with images of foreign cities and capitals—I could be assigned to U.S. Embassies and Consulates all around the world! Three weeks in Naples, a month in New Delhi, a quick weekend assignment in Reykjavik. All that stood between me and this life of adventure was a couple of personality and language aptitude tests to be administered by the U.S. Department of State in Washington, D.C.

The personality test was an assessment, and I felt that I did very well. Then came the language aptitude test—an agonizing oral exam where I pressed buttons to match sounds and tried to twist my tongue into impossible phrases, each one worse than the last.

Of course, it was quickly determined that I had absolutely no aptitude for foreign languages. My application was thrown out and all I had was the boring finance job that left me even more despondent than before.

The word "failure" hung over my head: I did not get into the Foreign Service. I didn't know where to go or what to do next. I thought about my job, and how different it was in reality than what'd I'd imagined it would be. In short, my entire life was beginning to look like a failure.

Yet, growing up on a cattle ranch had instilled in me a strong sense of persistence and determination. If something didn't work out right the first time, Plan B was quickly called into action. If cattle needed to be fed or watered (which usually meant life or death for them) I would keep at it until I found a way to keep moving forward and get the job done, no matter how long it took.

After failing the Foreign Service, I realized that I needed to put Plan B into action in my own life and refocus on what other options were out there for me. I wasn't going to wallow in self-pity. Since I had already researched U.S. Government jobs, I knew I also qualified for the FBI. I submitted the application. Six months later, I was in the FBI New Agents Training Academy at Quantico, VA.

I have never looked back.

Successful leaders are those who are good at Plan B. Why? Because by trying and failing, we learn what doesn't work—and with that comes the knowledge we need to understand what will work.

At the heart of Plan B is multiple iterations; multiple attempts that get fine-tuned with each iteration. Where there is a will, there is a way. Our will is stronger than our failure—and ultimately, our will is what lifts us up from failure and into success.

LESSONS LEARNED

Find gratitude and redefine "failure"

There have been many times in both my personal life and career when I was grateful for Plan B and the opportunities it gave me to keep moving forward when Plan A had failed.

Great leaders, from whatever organization or walk of life, tend to repeatedly cite one specific personal failure when explaining their success. Usually, the failure was one that was traumatic and difficult to transcend. Filled with desperation, they felt as though they'd hit rock bottom. As Warren Bennis said, "It's as if that moment the iron entered their soul; that moment created the resilience that leaders need."

Failure is a word freighted with negative connotations. We are so preoccupied with success and making money that we don't even know how to have conversations about how to keep moving forward when overcome with adversity. Instead, we place immense pressure on ourselves, and others, to focus only on success.

Many of us have experienced setbacks and failure in our careers as we moved toward that sweet spot of status and salary. After we find that sweet spot, something interesting happens to leaders who are not self-reflective enough to keep moving forward—we stop at success.

Too often, "success" is simply mediocrity. It's where we stop on our way to being the person we really wanted to be. We are smart, talented, and full of untapped potential—and too afraid to move into the discomfort of the unknown and push our boundaries. Why? We're afraid of failure.

Stay bold

Somewhere on the path to status and accomplishment, we've lost the bold and adventurous spirit that is willing to play with ideas, risk failure, remain positive, and bounce back with even more enthusiasm. We've lost our ability to discover, ignite, and break through our own self-limiting barriers.

Whereas fear and timidity are the usual cause of failure, failure can also come from a bold and adventuresome spirit. In exuberance, excitement and optimism, we push our boundaries to the point that we fail. However, we know that this sort of failure only motivates us to learn more about the very thing that has defeated us. It's a kind of failure that can actually serve us greatly.

The key is to not linger too long on anything that clearly isn't working. This means failing frequently. Only by trying many different things will you find the way that points to the best future. Repeated failure will build mental toughness and show you with absolute clarity how you must move forward if you are to succeed. It's actually a curse to have everything go right when you first start out because you will start to believe you have the golden touch . . . and when you do inevitably fail, you'll be demoralized.

Lose the shame

We are afraid of failure because, essentially, we have a fear of shame. Most of us are not motivated to avoid failing because we cannot manage the basic emotions of disappointment or frustration that may emerge; instead, we feel deep shame that we are imperfect—and vulnerable.

Shame was a hard emotion for me to shed because it got to the core of my ego, my identity and my self-esteem. Shame was damaging because it caused me to avoid the psychological threats associated with failing. The most insidious threat was believing the lie that I was unworthy of love and respect just as I was—faults and all.

It has taken a great deal of my life to discover not only what I'm good at, but how I find value and meaning in my work. To make these discoveries, I've had to fail—rather spectacularly at times. This is what I've learned: failure brings clarity.

Failure offers the gift of bringing priorities into focus. If something doesn't hold value for you, then giving up and moving on to something different does no more than prick your pride. If, however, you risk losing something important, you will work hard and do what it takes to tackle the obstacle that stands between you and success.

If we want to energize our leadership, we must cultivate the courage to risk failure in order to move toward the things in life that produce value and meaning.

KEY QUESTIONS

- How has a Plan B in your life led to your success?

- How has a failure brought you clarity in the direction you wanted to go?

- How do you define success?

ACTION STEPS

Here are three action steps that will help you look at failure in a different way:

1. Start as a beginner

The beginner's mind does not need to prove or disprove anything. It has the humility to simultaneously hold "what I do know" and "what I don't know." Holding this kind of tension leads to wisdom, not just easy answers.

The more accomplished we are at something, the harder it is to learn. Once we become experts in our field, the need to learn is no longer urgent or necessary. This, in turn, increases the likelihood that we will fuse our skill level with our identity.

When we allow ourselves the luxury of trial and error, like a child learning to walk, we experience a feel-good neurological response that can be stronger than the ego. When tackling new and difficult challenges, we experience a rush of adrenaline, a hormone that makes us feel confident and motivated.

2. Learn the right lesson

The only thing worse than a failure is someone who fails, and then fails to learn from the experience. Reflect, explain what you've learned, then show how the experience has made you stronger.

As leaders who are looking for ways to energize our leadership, the story we tell ourselves is important. We need to validate our learning. One way we can do this is by looking at our decisions as experiments, not final choices. This gives us permission to look at aspects of our life as a petri dish that provides new insight into what works, or doesn't, and then move from there. If we insist upon brushing aside our failures, we cannot learn the right lesson from them.

3. Use failure to identify your blind spots

Failures provide us with vital information about our psychological blind spots that we would not have recognized before. We tend to make a mistake and repeat it in endless variations, both in life and work. That is the definition of a working blind spot: a repetitive error we don't see but keep making. Imagine having a crystal ball that tells you what mistakes you're most likely to make in the future. You would happily watch out for them and correct them before they happened. Failure is that crystal ball.

In a world that desperately needs leaders to discover, ignite and break through to claim their potential, we need to see failure as an opportunity to learn valuable truths about ourselves.

By LaRae Quy

www.LaRaeQuy.com

"The way you deal with failure determines how you'll achieve success. #EnergizedLeaders"

14: When Confronted with Challenges, Have Serious Fun

Everyone remembers moments from childhood where everything seemed carefree and the possibilities were endless. One of my favorite memories is the fresh smell after a good rain on the farm. I don't think there's a sweeter, more enlivening smell. And as a kid, that smell meant the fun was about to begin. After a good rain, our graveled yard was filled with puddles galore. We slipped on our rubber boots, bolted out the door, and tried our hardest to empty every puddle as we jumped from one to the next.

For all of us, childhood fun ignited a spirit of laughter, imagination and boundless opportunity discovery. Fun delivers a beautiful simplicity; clearing boundaries and cleansing spirits.

As we get older, complexity edges in. As we move from the playground to the workplace, seriousness consumes our endeavors and occupies our time. We take on many responsibilities, not only in what we do but in who we support and take care of.

I was fortunate that, during my career, I got to experience a Childhood 2.0 – in the glory days of the dot com boom. Our workdays were full of fun, play, creativity and the energy of limitless possibility. We brought to life many creative marketing campaigns and worked with cool people energized by the promise of big dreams. Venture funds flowed into companies with ideas, little revenue and boundless upside.

It was, in fact, a marketing "arms race" of sorts. How creative could we be to get a prospect's attention? How could we "out-creative" our competitors and win the account? One of our best campaigns was Presley-themed, and included Pink Cadillac packaging, a swiveling pelvis Elvis Presley clock, and a drawing for an expense-paid trip to Memphis and Graceland. Not only was it fun, but it worked!

As we all know, that era was short-lived and came to a crashing halt. The bottom fell out, and

I went from brainstorming new concepts one day to giving pink notices to half the company the next. Job opportunities were zilch and the job market in the Silicon Hills of Austin, Texas, was barren.

Eventually, we recovered and many found new work as the economy began rising again. But reflecting on those days of boom, burst and bust in the dotcom era, I realized I learned an important leadership lesson in—maybe —the importance of tension and balance.

I like to look at it through the metaphor of a trampoline. A trampoline is potentially dangerous and accidents are just waiting to happen. You have a number of powerful springs and a taut, firm tarp that could easily launch you too high or cause you to lose control and injure yourself. But a trampoline also is fun. As we climb on, we sense the bounce in our movements, and notice that the more effort we put into it, the higher we go. As others join in, a flow and synchronicity of movement takes over, and all seems good and effortless (just like in childhood).

And here is the interesting tension: the higher we jump, the greater our exuberance and sense of joy – but the greater the care we exercise because of the potential for accidents. In this sense, the more fun we're having, the more care we're taking – and that is the key to it all. Play for fun and release but also for seriousness and competitiveness. Essentially, let go and yet grow more aware. This is serious fun, because the tension between the two clears the air and gives rise to new ideas and thinking.

During the dotcom bust, I had lost my sense of fun and was seriously imbalanced.

I regained a forgotten spark. Introducing play in team events at work, and in my personal life, helped me recover. There was a ripple effect, and I felt its positive impact.

LESSONS LEARNED

Although trampolines are mostly thought of for kids' play, they're also used in competition (think gymnasts or astronauts-in-training). This juxtaposition gives an interesting perspective on the balance needed for leadership:

Play with competitiveness

Our society is shifting: the sharing economy is booming and our work has become more open and collaborative. Competitiveness is key, as it keeps our skills and minds sharp. However, when it comes to solving problems, we find ways to leverage the intelligence and insights of different individuals. There is great strength in diversity and collaboration.

But play is essential to maintaining balance. Taking my team to a movie with a strong story helps them flesh out new ideas or concepts in their work. Playing games sharpens our problem-solving skills and empowers new, creative approaches to business challenges.

Our sense of competitiveness shifts from individuals being in direct competition with each other, to individuals harnessing the energy of competition to better solve a problem and get the best result. The infusion of play focuses our competitiveness on the right collaborative areas. Play lowers our guard with one another and encourages a way to interact, think, solve and move initiatives forward in a more productive, energized way.

Fun with seriousness

Our days are still the same 24 hours they were 50 years ago, but we spend a larger percentage of our time doing work. This translates to a more serious mind. Without fun, we get bogged down in drudgery. Our smiles turn to gritted teeth, and our laughter disappears.

Seriousness without fun dulls our creative edge. We focus on the task at hand, becoming machine-like.

Fun can be simple. With my teams, I hold a monthly "bananas and coffee" meeting. The combination sets a tone of fun and interaction. Everyone comes with a more open attitude and a ready smile.

Fun builds organizational culture. Some companies measure their team members' happiness and have implemented a Gross Happiness Index. Warby Parker asks their employees each week to rate their happiness on a scale of 1 to 10. Organizations like this understand the importance of having the right mix of fun and seriousness to keep people balanced and, most importantly, engaged in the workplace.

Release with tension

Not all tension is bad. Tension stretches us. It heightens our awareness of a given problem, its solution and everything in between. Yet, without a release, something will snap and people will get hurt (in feelings, emotions, isolation and untapped insights).

When the right release happens, people bounce higher. The right release restores a rhythm between team members and we find synchronized flow in upward movement.

Release can come in the form of fun or play as well as in taking a break, going for a walk, meditating or other mindfulness activities. It can also come from just remembering to breathe. Taking deep breaths during tense moments and keeping a natural breathing cadence will keep you centered.

Tension should not be ignored though. When work is addressing a critical issue in which sides are clear, I try to embrace the tension with a growth mindset, meaning what I learn from another's perspective and where can we find the common ground. Doing this leverages the tension to achieve real results. Afterwards, I like to take a playful break or deliver some appropriate joke to release the tension and restore a mindful balance.

When thinking about the right balance of having fun and doing work, remember a trampoline. Determine what will put a bounce in everyone's step. Think about what will keep operations tight and well-orchestrated. Lead in a way that keeps people moving in the right direction while still leaving room for creativity.

KEY QUESTIONS

- What signs point to an imbalance between release and tension?

- How does culture play a role in fun and play?

- As a leader, what is your responsibility in fun and play, and how are you allocating your time?

ACTION STEPS

Navigating a trampoline takes skill and focus along with a good sense of balance. Three key actions will energize your leadership and keep your team engaged:

1. Identify and use triggers to enhance your awareness

We learn about current events from newspapers and news sites. Within our industry, trade publications and blogs keep us abreast of trends. Listening to our sales, marketing, and customer support teams inform us of relevant and important information. We just need to identify the triggers to watch for, and then spend the time to discern and decide what to do next. Determine the key signs you want to be aware of, and then build in the watch points to trigger an engaging, refreshing action.

2. Define and develop your creative culture

Defining your organizational culture will reveal the direction and the values to embrace and demonstrate consistently. If fun and play are removed completely from your culture, talent, creativity and innovation will dry up and your leadership bench will become vacant. Fostering the right culture will generate the right cultural flow to keep everyone more engaged and working toward building a company that endures through generations.

3.   Lead with a smile

As a leader, set the example. If you never laugh, you won't hear much laughter from others. If people don't see you enjoying yourself, their attitudes may sour.

Intention and influence are key elements of leading well. Effective leaders set an intention to make fun and play a priority, and envision how both will foster the development of leaders, aid the recruitment of new team members and create an engaging work culture. Good leaders also are talented influencers – they identify key working relationships and provide informal opportunities for these bonds to strengthen.

In fun and play, leaders carry a responsibility – personally and organizationally. The result is mutual growth and fulfillment.

By Jon Mertz

www.thindifference.com

"Fun delivers a beautiful simplicity; clearing boundaries and cleansing spirits. #EnergizedLeaders"

15: Lead with Curiosity

The staff I met, after being recruited on short notice to help an organization resolve an internal team issue, did not look very happy to see me. The company was in the midst of a ten-week long restructuring process and, although the underlying reasons for the change were layered and complex, what the team knew for sure was that roles, titles and positions were all in upheaval.

This particular team, during this process, had suffered a complete loss of designated leadership staff (against the backdrop of this already-uncertain climate). I was asked to stabilize and lead the team, pending the recruitment of a new manager and some additional part-time support staff.

The staff were very bruised emotionally, angry at the way they had been treated, extremely concerned by the 'them vs. us' gulf created by the process and, consequently, enormously distrustful of the senior management team. They also clearly suspected that hidden in the process was a change planned for their team, which had been regarded as the most successful across the organization.

I'd seen this before. Many times. I knew just how damaging—emotionally and mentally— these situations can be, and how they can negatively impact performance. Now, just as before, I was curious to understand just how far-reaching the impact had been on the team, on staff as individuals, and also on their current levels of performance. I also wanted to discover what was needed to restore their self-belief and trust in both the restructuring process and the direction of change.

In the previous change situations, I'd heavily relied on my curiosity to help discern 'reality' from some imagined (often speculative) state of being; to help build a 'bigger picture,' in which I could place my own position in relation to other colleagues; and to gather better intelligence around purpose and direction.

My sense of curiosity has always driven me to seek—and find—greater clarity. I've done this by asking powerful questions, when others might have taken the safe route and been more conservative. I find that simplicity is very effective. For instance, just asking 'Why?' can help reveal a deeper understanding of intent and purpose. Inquisitiveness often breeds more questions than answers, although, as an iterative approach, it is often ideal for gathering a lot of information quickly. In difficult change situations, I've seen that the more information available, the more transparent the process, and the more likely that participants will adjust sooner.

I want to better understand those around me. My listening skills are greatly improved by my curiosity. Better listening skills lead to deeper insights and enlightenment into situations and perspectives. And it goes far in remedying, smoothing out or otherwise helping stabilize a restructuring or change process. Leaders can glean a lot through the body language, tone of voice and eye contact of those they're working with. Engaging empathetically also enabled me to feel more valued and cared for, and to share this with others.

Drawing on my curiosity allows me to suspend my assumptions and keep an open mind. It helps me to get to know what my colleagues are really thinking. I gain better insight into their critical thinking processes and secure wider perspectives on issues of the day. This helps me to develop more effective listening skills and, as a result, deepens my ability to learn. Demonstrating this learning builds goodwill—which helps me and those I care about to thrive, not just survive—in difficult change processes.

So in that room, with all those faces looking at me apprehensively, I began with curiosity. I addressed them in an open and transparent style, driving deep into their responses. I shared my approach, so they could see that there was both a basis for and a method to it. We shared and discussed and voiced concerns and opinions. I made sure curiosity and empathetic engagement underpinned the entire conversation.

What emerged helped clarify the process for the staff, quell fears and show that everyone was in this together. In particular, I was able to quickly assess where each team member felt they were within the current scenario, and identify actions to support them in working through their response to the change agenda. We explored how they might do this more effectively. I led them in defining and then implementing some demonstrable actions that began to restore their faith in themselves, and which enabled them to begin thinking about the future in a more positive light. Within a few days, their trust and confidence in me and my leadership had grown by leaps and bounds, and they let me help them move forward with more optimism, clarity and energy.

LESSONS LEARNED

Curiosity creates energy

This recent experience was enlightening not just for the power of the process and how quickly it took shape, but also because it truly energized me and the staff. Curiosity energizes leaders because it delivers fundamental impact on your success as a leader. It enabled me to be receptive, reflective, perceptive and open—all qualities that demonstrate a strongly authentic leadership approach.

The team's response to my curiosity was extraordinary. Very quickly, tensions eased, balance was restored, focus was recovered and laughter and light-hearted banter filled our team base. We sparked off each other and over the ten weeks moved from a state of despondency to a focused consideration of what was needed for the future and even a beginning plan for achieving those things. Along the way, we managed to maintain the front-line delivery of services with minimal disruption and delivered a major event, involving over 90 young people and staff, which had looked in serious jeopardy when I took up the assignment.

Curiosity drives change

I recognize that curiosity requires courage—a willingness to take risks, a desire to be better as a person and leader, and the drive to cultivate a bigger 'world view.' It also requires a willingness to embrace feedback, to look for insight, to seek out clarity, to understand how people are experiencing 'reality,' and to stay focused on values and purpose.

Curiosity sparks learning

As an energized leader my core focus is on learning – about myself, about those with whom I work, and about the organization of which I am a part. To enhance that learning, I remain willing to play with ideas, risk failure, remain upbeat, and bounce back with even more enthusiasm. Doing this during my recent assignment helped our team discover a better 'reality,' reignited their enthusiasm and passion for their work, and enabled them to break through their self-limiting beliefs and achieve things that others thought unlikely!

KEY QUESTIONS

- What help do you need to be a more curious leader?

- What do you see as the next steps in developing your curiosity?

- What does the power of curiosity invite you to do in your role as an energized leader?

ACTION STEPS

As a curious and energized leader your role is to develop your people, as well as yourself. It is not simply about telling them what to do. Having the courage to show curiosity, by asking powerful questions, will go a long way to helping you to accomplish this. By practicing curiosity you will discover new things about yourself, about the people and the processes around you, and about how you can lead differently—and more effectively.

Here are three action steps to help you to employ curiosity more effectively:

1. Ask powerful questions

These can be as simple as 'Why?' Powerful questions show that you are willing to explore diverse points of view, that you are aware of potential areas of conflict, that demonstrate that your own views aren't always the best ideas, and that you are interested in what and how your team members think.

I recommend both making questioning a key goal and offering your team permission on this. This helps to test assumptions, develops Stephen Covey's principle of 'first seek to understand ... and then be understood,' and it creates many opportunities for learning.

2. Practice really listening to others

Do this by making eye contact and nodding, by reflecting back what you are hearing, and by asking powerful follow-up questions that show you were paying attention and truly hearing what the other person had to say. Acting on what you hear also clearly demonstrates that you heard them!

3. Get uncomfortable

Do something you dislike and note three unexpected things you learn from it. Doing this helped me to tap into my openness and willingness to learn, and enabled many new learning experiences.

Alternately, practice like a beginner, taking on new challenges and roles that stretch your thinking and practice. I have found throughout my career that moving into an uncomfortable space often brings new learning to the surface, so my advice would be to feel the fear and take the risk.

As an energized and growing leader, remember that you will not have all the answers, nor should you be expected to. I believe, from my own experience, that relinquishing control, suspending judgment, holding back on providing instant solutions, and embracing ignorance (the lack of knowledge or insight) all set the stage for powerful sharing, input and learning.

Using curiosity is absolutely essential for differentiating those who seek to lead authentically, for dealing with relentless change, for overcoming the myth that leaders are 'all knowing and all doing,' for building strong relationships with others, and for illuminating needs, building rapport and establishing trust.

Most of all, I can personally attest that growing as a curious, energized leader will deliver better business results, improved employee well-being and engagement, and enhanced individual, team and organizational impact.

By John Thurlbeck

www.wearconsulting.co.uk

"Curiosity energizes leaders because it delivers fundamental impact on their success as a leader. #EnergizedLeaders"

16: Positivity Is Always Possible

I made my way through the buzzing crowd to find the room where I would be speaking. My eyes caught curious glances and some raised eyebrows. Some people passing by me asked who I was. This was an opportunity I'd wanted to do for the last year. There were countless meetings and upward approvals needed from leadership to give me the green light. I kept up hope that it would work out because I knew my message of positivity was something this group needed to hear.

Up at the podium, as I looked out to the group of about 100 people, I asked myself, "Will they really connect with the message of positivity? Will they get it?"

If this had been a group of CEOs or entrepreneurs, I wouldn't have been too worried. They know how important positivity is. This group, however, was not considered to be highly motivated or have the outward appearance of having lots of opportunity in their future. This was a large group of high school students. Not just high-schoolers, but high-risk high-schoolers who were most likely not going to graduate high school at the rate they were going. Many had already been in the juvenile system, and some were surely just one infraction away from jail time.

You can prepare as best as you can for a presentation like this, but you really have to be on your toes because you never know what a group like this will throw at you. But I had faith. I knew there was positivity inside of them. At the very least, I knew positivity was possible.

Standing there before them, I realized just how far positivity had brought me and also how, at one time, I wasn't too different from these kids. I came from a small town with very limited opportunities. At times I doubted that life had much more to offer. I could have resigned myself to that outlook and just let life happen to me. But I decided early on that I wanted new, exciting experiences. I focused on my long-term goal of doing something different. And so, looking to that future, I packed my bags and left my hometown.

Fortunately I had a mentor early on who inspired me to think for myself and encouraged me to create my own destiny. My mentor gave me motivation and hope that no matter where I wanted to go in life, I could do it, but that I must focus on the things I can control.

Positivity has to come from within but it also has to be realistic. Being positive about things that are fantastical or far-fetched do nothing but set you up for failure or disappointment. But it is possible to know one's capabilities and skills and be realistic and positive at the same time. There is great energy in this positivity and it guides all of your future endeavors. We all have the basic resources for positivity in our own achievements and capabilities. As long as we can maintain focus on those factors we can control, positivity is never out of range.

I knew these students had positivity reserves still untapped. They had the raw material and knowledge with which to build a positive future. Yes, they would connect. Yes, they would understand.

LESSONS LEARNED

Positivity is a choice

From early on in my own life, I learned that no matter what challenges may come, it is my personal choice to focus on the positive things and what I can do in life. The kids at the high school definitely had some challenges in front of them, but from what I heard and saw as the day progressed, they knew they wanted something different than what they currently had. I knew it couldn't hurt to keep repeating that they needed to consciously do positive things themselves in order to achieve a good life. They needed to see beyond the challenges, and look to the future with positivity. There's an old saying that the best way to learn is to teach, and presenting this message of positivity that day reinvigorated my stance of taking responsibility for my own happiness and growth. Just like my mentor had inspired me all those years ago, working with these kids inspired me all over.

Achieving Goals Take Time

The big goals in life take time. We have to work hard. Sweat. Re-strategize. Not every day is going to be a perfect day and it may seem like forever before we get things done. So in order to keep a positive mindset, I am in charge of motivating myself. And I must focus on what I do accomplish. Focus on my wins. And just as I would do for my personal goals, I must reward myself positively when making small, professional achievements. When I gift myself a reward for achieving a goal, it will keep me pumped up and energized to keep moving forward toward achieving the next goal . . . and the one after that.

Find your uniqueness and nurture yourself

Step into your greatness by taking ownership of what is unique about you. Today is a brand new day. Keep your eyes and mind open to opportunities and possibilities. The opportunity to start something over, do something new or do things better than you thought you ever could in your leadership starts today!

This is a strategy for long-term success. So is making sure to take care of yourself. Along the way, I learned that if I wanted to be successful and positive in my daily professional life, I must take care of myself on the inside. Not just once in a while. It needs to be a daily thing. A habit. A mindset. A way of life. A shift towards being inspired each day of my life. So I design a plan of things I love to do to take good care of myself in life. When I feel good and positive on the inside, it translates to other good things on the outside.

KEY QUESTIONS

- What positive things are you going to do for yourself each day, to take good care of yourself?

- How will you take those positive, personal habits and translate them into your personal leadership?

- How will you know you have succeeded in keeping positive each day personally and professionally?

ACTION STEPS

1. **Act on what you can do**

If you want to be a positive leader, you must focus on the things that you have control over in life. Those are the things you can change. What can you change in your daily routine to make things better? Don't waste your time or energy on things that are out of your control. Focus on moving forward, on action and results, on things that you can do. Think of five things you can do now that will help move you in a more positive direction.

2. Practice gratitude

The best leaders are confident but humble leaders. As quickly as you can rise, you can fall. So what is it that you can do to keep a positive mindset in the course of sometimes challenging days? Focus on gratitude, all the things and people that you have in your life. So as you start each day, think about what is positive in your career and personal life. Have deep appreciation for everything that you accomplish and enjoy in life. Have gratitude for the opportunity to live and breathe and to make a difference each day. We all have things to be grateful for and to appreciate in life. The key is to focus on it.

Day and night. So we don't lose perspective. Make a habit of taking five minutes at the beginning and end of your day to mentally review things in your life that you're grateful for.

3. Engage with Positive People

If you want to be the best, you must surround yourself with the best. Let go of toxic people in your life and fill it with inspiring, positive people!

Positivity is one of the keys to living a successful, happy, professional life. And the absolutely awesome thing is, if you need to change your mindset, you can start today. You have the power to be miserable or positive as a leader and life is really too short to just be enduring your career. Forgive yourself right now for any mistakes you've made. Every experience was absolutely necessary to bring your life to where you are today. And remember, a healthy person on the inside is going to translate to a healthy leader on the outside.

You deserve great happiness and success and you are definitely too blessed to be stressed. Positivity isn't about saying everything is always perfect, but it *is* about enjoying your life. We have limited time in life and worrying about things you can't control or do is just not effective. So when making the choice on how to live your life, think about people that you really look up to. What characteristics do they have? What do you love about their attitude? What is it that inspires you about them? I bet positivity is one of them!

By Cynthia Bazin

www.smartchic.me

"Positivity is always possible. There is great energy in positivity and it guides all your future endeavors. #EnergizedLeaders"

Afterword

We hope you have been energized with our stories and lessons and are now ready to explore your own leadership. Delve deeper into the sections that matter to you most and that speak to where you are in your leadership today. Discover. Ignite. Break Through. Remember, you can lead from anywhere and you now have 16 new insights to grow your leadership story.

We also invite you to ask the authors questions you may have about any of the topics or insights through our Facebook page, Energize Your Leadership, or contacting the authors directly. At the end of each chapter is the author's contact information and we would be thrilled to continue the conversation on how to Energize Your Leadership.

We would like to thank LaRae Quy for her dedication and leadership in keeping all of us on track throughout this book project.

We would also like to give thanks to Dan Forbes for his support in the early stages of the book.

A big thank you goes to our editor, Jennifer Downey, who guided us with her extraordinary writing skills.

About the Authors

SUSAN MAZZA - FLORIDA

CEO of Clarus Works, Susan Mazza is a business coach and motivational speaker who works with leaders and their teams to transform their performance, relationships and work environment from acceptable to exceptional. Named one of the Top 100 Thought Leaders by Trust Across America/ Trust Around the World in 2013/2015, Susan co-authored The Character-Based Leader and is the founder/author of the highly acclaimed blog
www.RandomActsofLeadership.com

TERRI KLASS - NEW YORK

Terri Klass is a Leadership Training Consultant and Speaker who partners with organizations to create cultures of empowerment and develop future leadership. She delivers highly successful leadership workshops and is a speaker and author of articles about working with the different generations in the workplace. Terri has an MBA and is Myers-Briggs certified. Learn more about Terri at **www.terriklassconsulting.com**

BARRY SMITH - OREGON

Founder of Building What Matters, llc and a founding member of The John Maxwell Team. Barry is an international Coach, Speaker and Author focused on Leadership and Personal Development. Barry believes in building what matters and what matters is people. Author of Leadership by Invitation. Learn more about Barry at **www.buildingwhatmatters.com**

TONY VENGROVE - CONNECTICUT

Tony Vengrove is Founder of Miles Finch Innovation, creator of the Idea Climate Equation®, and an innovation omnivore. His career spans NYC ad agency and Fortune 500 brand marketing and innovation roles, which arms him with a unique general management

perspective of leading innovation and change. Learn more about Tony at
www.milesfinchinnovation.com

KARIN HURT - MARYLAND

Karin Hurt, CEO of Let's Grow Leaders, is a leadership speaker, author, consultant, and MBA professor. She's a former Verizon Wireless executive with two decades of diverse cross-functional experience in sales, customer service and HR. She helps leaders get better results by building deeper trust and connection with their teams. Learn more about Karin at
www.letsgrowleaders.com/about

ALLI POLIN – AUSTRALIA / WASHINGTON D.C.

Alli Polin, CPCC, ACC, is a former senior executive with deep experience in change management and organization development. Now a coach, speaker and facilitator, she is driven to help people engage more purposefully at the intersection of life and leadership. To learn more about Alli and her work visit
www.breaktheframe.com

CAROL DOUGHERTY - ILLINOIS

Carol Dougherty is the President of Delta Consulting Group, LLC. She helps the next generation of leaders develop their potential by building skills in communication, time management, decision making, and leadership. Learn more about Carol at
www.delta-group-llc.com

DANIEL BUHR - MINNESOTA

Daniel Buhr has been an EHS information analyst in the Fortune 500 corporate world for over 27 years. He is also a leadership developer, promoting the PAR principle that in leadership we each have the Permission, Ability and Responsibility to lead. You can find him on social media as @Cybuhr or at **www.Cybuhr.com**

LALITA RAMAN - HONG KONG

Lalita Raman is an Executive and Leadership Coach, Trainer and Speaker who partners with people, business and organizations to develop, empower and assist them in delivering results that they seek. She delivers leadership and sales training workshops and assists in discovering and developing the talent of organizations and individuals. Learn more about Lalita at **www.transitionsintl.com**

CHERY GEGELMAN – SAUDI ARABIA

Chery Gegelman was once a frustrated visionary that learned how to instigate and lead system-wide change from the middle and the edge of organizations. Today she speaks and consults with people and organizations that are learning to lead through change to growth. Learn more about Chery at **www.consultgiana.com**

DR. HODA MAALOUF - LEBANON

Dr. Hoda Maalouf was born and raised in Beirut, Lebanon. She moved to the UK for graduate studies at Imperial College, earning a Ph.D. in Communication Engineering. Hoda currently teaches, advises students and serves as head of the Computer Science Department at Notre Dame University, Lebanon. Learn more about Hoda at **www.HodaMaalouf.com**

SCOTT MABRY - TENNESSEE

Scott Mabry is a former school teacher and experienced senior executive with a passion for helping others find meaning in their life and work. He still teaches every day and shares his thoughts on how we can "bring our soul to work" at **www.soul2work.com**

LARAE QUY - CALIFORNIA

LaRae Quy is a former counterintelligence and undercover FBI agent. She speaks and coaches on how to develop the mental strength to control emotions, behavior, and thinking that lead to personal and professional success. Learn more about LaRae at **www.LaRaeQuy.com**

JON MERTZ - TEXAS

Jon Mertz is one of the 2014 Top 100 Thought Leaders in Trustworthy Business and writes to empower Millennials to become conscious leaders, build stronger teams, and lead a richer life. Learn more about Jon at
www.thindifference.com

JOHN THURLBECK - UNITED KINGDOM

Founder of Wear Consulting Limited, John is a super-connector – an international facilitator, trainer and coach focused on critically transforming relationships, building extraordinary networks, developing energized leadership and enabling powerful organizational change. Learn more about John at **www.wearconsulting.co.uk**

CYNTHIA BAZIN - CALIFORNIA

Cynthia Bazin is a motivational speaker, expert writer and mentor who has 20+ years of leadership experience. She is an Investigations Expert and former Private Investigator who owns SmartChic, a premier mentoring company for women. She empowers women with laser-focused strategies so they can live their most successful and happiest life. Learn more about Cynthia at **www.smartchic.me**

19604168R00131

Made in the USA
Middletown, DE
27 April 2015